English - Cantonese

My first Picture Dictionary

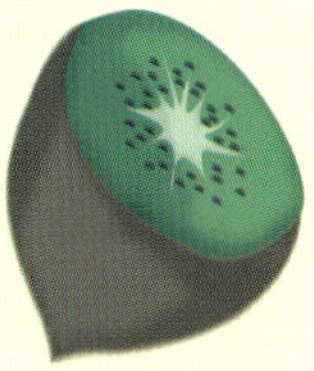

Designed and edited by : Maria Watson
Translated by : Antonia Chan

Biblio Bee Publications

English - Cantonese
My First Picture Dictionary

ISBN: 978 1 912826 33 9

Published by
Biblio Bee Publications
An imprint of **Star Books**
56, Langland Crescent, Stanmore HA7 1NG, U.K.
Tel: 020 8900 2640, Fax: 020 3621 6116,
email: sales@starbooksuk.com, www.bilingualbooks.co.uk

First Edition : 2022

Printed at : Star Print-O-Bind, New Delhi-110 020 (India)

This dictionary has been published in the following languages:
Albanian, Amharic, Arabic, Bengali, Bulgarian, Cantonese, Croatian, Czech, Dari, Farsi French, Gujarati, Haitian Creole, Hindi, Hungarian, Italian, Korean, Latvian, Levantine Lithuanian, Mandarin, Pashto, Polish, Portuguese, Punjabi, Romanian, Russian, Slovak Spanish, Tagalog, Tamil, Turkish, Urdu and Vietnamese.

Aa

actor

男演員
naam^4 jin^2 jyun^4

actress

女演員
neoi^5 jin^2 jyun^4

adult

成人 sing^4 jan^4

aeroplane
US English **airplane**

飛機 fei^1 gei^1

air conditioner

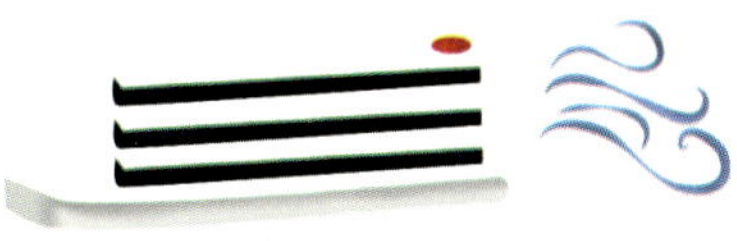

冷氣機
laang^5 hei^3 gei^1

air hostess
US English **flight attendant**

空中小姐
hung^1 zung^1 siu^2 ze^2

airport

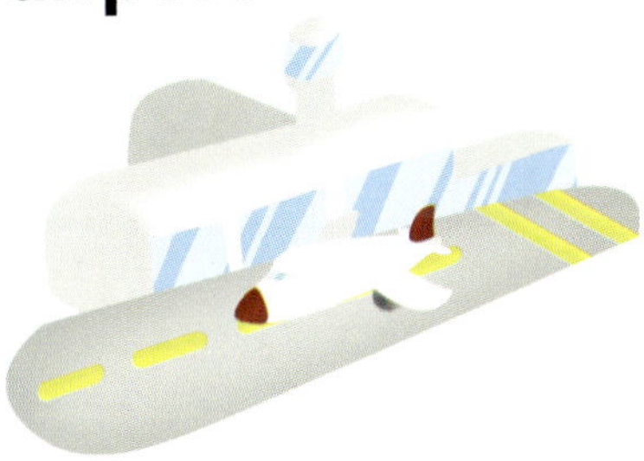

機場 gei^1 coeng^4

album

相簿 soeng^2 bou^2

almond

杏仁 hang^6 jan^4

alphabet

字母 zi^6 mou^5

ambulance

救護車 gau^3 wu^6 ce^1

a b c d e f g h i j k l m n o p q r s t u v w x y z

angel

天使 tin1 si2

animal

動物 dung6 mat6

ankle

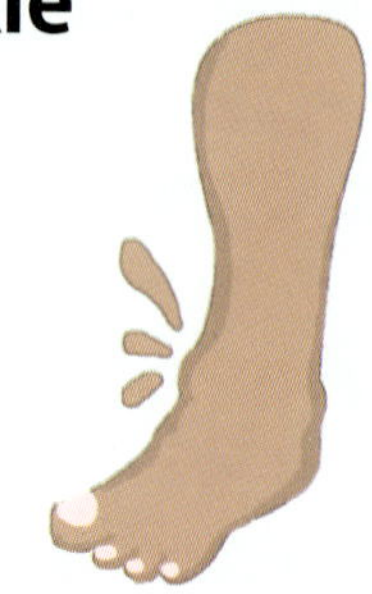

腳腕 goek3 wun2

ant

螞蟻 maa5 ngai5

antelope

羚羊 ling4 joeng4

antenna

天線 tin1 sin3

apartment

住宅大廈 zyu6 zaak2 daai6 haa6

ape

猿 jyun4

apple

蘋果 ping4 gwo2

apricot

杏桃 hang6 tou4

apron

圍裙 wai4 kwan2

aquarium

水族館 seoi2 zuk6 gun2

archery

射箭 se6 zin3

architect

建築師 gin3 zuk1 si1

arm

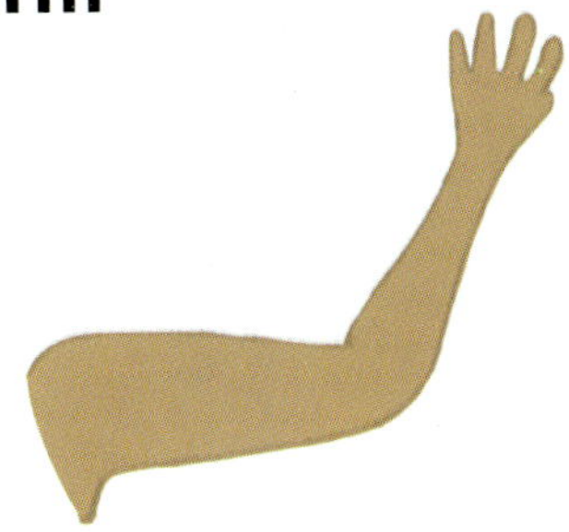

手臂 sau2 bei3

armour

US English **armor**

盔甲 kwai1 gaap3

arrow

箭 zin3

artist

藝術家
ngai6 seot6 gaa1

asparagus

蘆荀 lou4 seon1

astronaut

太空人
taai3 hung1 jan4

astronomer

天文學家
tin1 man4 hok6 gaa1

athlete

運動員
wan6 dung6 jyun4

atlas

地圖 dei6 tou4

aunt

姨姨 ji1 ji1

author

作者 zok^{3} ze^{2}

automobile

汽車 hei^{3} ce^{1}

autumn

秋天 cau^{1} tin^{1}

avalanche

雪崩 syut^{3} bang^{1}

award

獎項 zoeng^{2} hong^{6}

axe

斧頭 fu^{2} tau^{4}

Bb

baby

嬰兒 jing^{1} ji^{4}

back

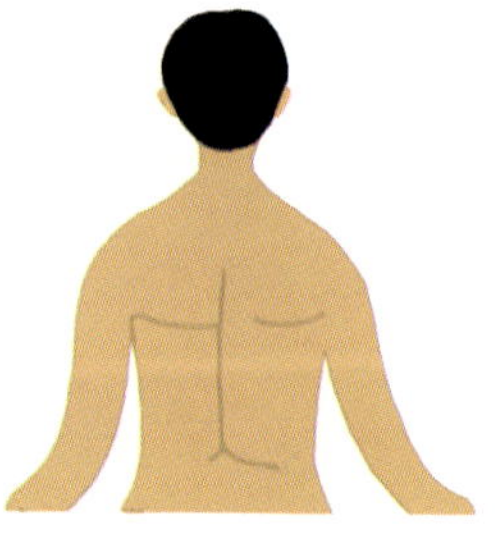

背脊 bui^{3} zek^{3}

bacon

煙肉 jin^{1} juk^{6}

badge

徽章 fai^{1} zoeng^{1}

badminton

羽毛球 jyu^{5} mou^{4} kau^{4}

bag

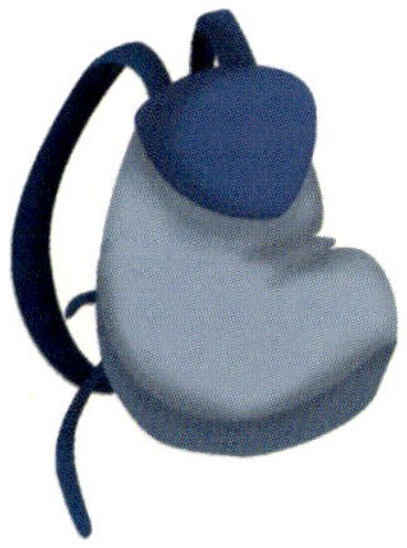

袋 doi^{2}

baker

烘焙師 hong^{3} bui^{6} si^{1}

balcony

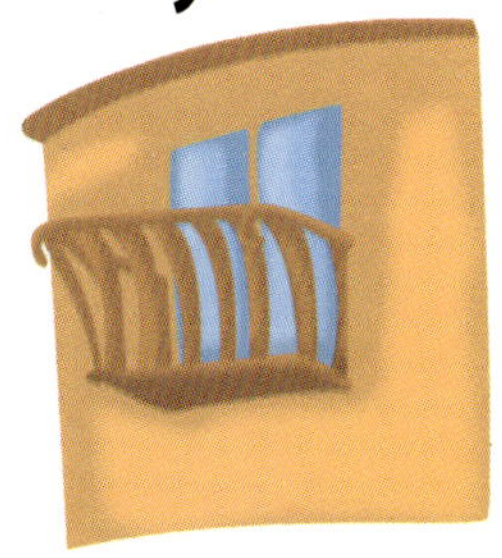

露台 lou^{6} toi^{4}

bald

禿頭 tuk^{1} tau^{4}

ball

球 kau^{4}

ballerina

芭蕾舞家
baa^{1} leoi^{4} mou^{5} gaa^{1}

balloon

氣球 hei^{3} kau^{4}

bamboo

竹 zuk^{1}

banana

香蕉 hoeng^{1} ziu^{1}

band

樂團 ngok^{6} tyun^{4}

bandage

繃帶 bang^{1} daai^{2}

barbeque

燒烤 siu^{1} haau^{1}

barn

穀倉 guk1 cong1

barrel

桶 tung2

baseball

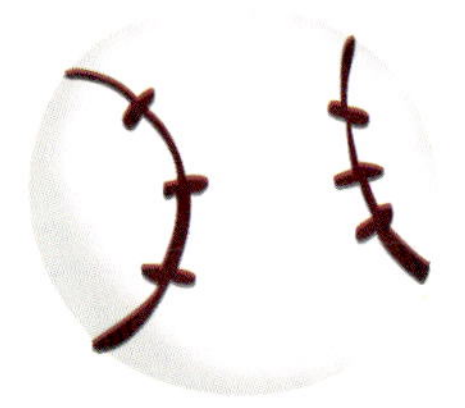

棒球 paang5 kau4

basket

籃 laam2

basketball

籃球 laam4 kau4

bat

蝙蝠 pin1 fuk1

bath

洗澡 sai2 cou3

battery

電池 din6 ci4

bay

港灣 gong2 waan1

beach

沙灘 saa1 taan1

beak

鳥嘴 niu5 zeoi2

bean

豆 dau2

bear

熊 hung^{4}

beard

鬍鬚 wu^{4} sou^{1}

bed

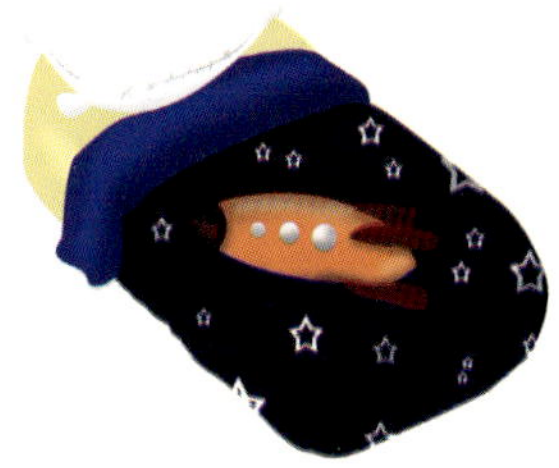

床 cong^{4}

bee

蜜蜂 mat^{6} fung^{1}

beetle

甲蟲 gaap^{3} cung^{4}

beetroot

紅菜頭 hung^{4} coi^{3} tau^{4}

bell

鈴 ling^{4}

belt

皮帶 pei^{4} daai^{2}

berry

莓 mui^{4}

bicycle

單車 daan^{1} ce^{1}

billiards
US English **pool**

桌球 coek^{3} kau^{4}

bin

垃圾桶 laap^{6} saap^{3} tung^{2}

bird

雀鳥 zoek^3 niu^5

biscuit

餅乾 beng^2 gon^1

black

黑色 hak^1 sik^1

blackboard

黑板 hak^1 baan^2

blanket

毛氈 mou^4 zin^1

blizzard

暴風雪
bou^6 fung^1 syut^3

blood

血 hyut^3

blue

藍色 laam^4 sik^1

boat

艇 teng^5

body

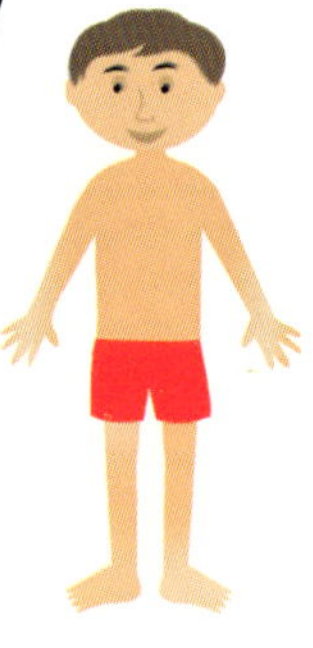

身體 san^1 tai^2

bone

骨頭 gwat^1 tau^4

book

書 syu^1

boot

靴 hoe1

bottle

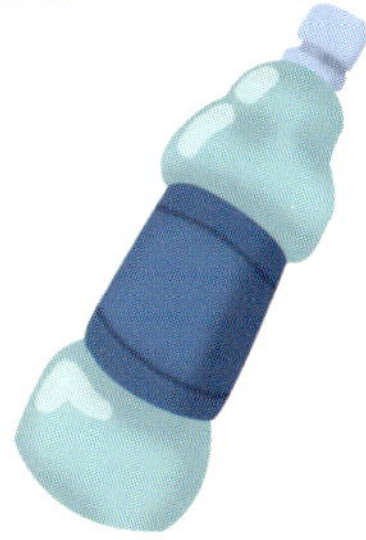

樽 zeon1

bow

蝴蝶結 wu4 dip6 git3

bowl

碗 wun2

box

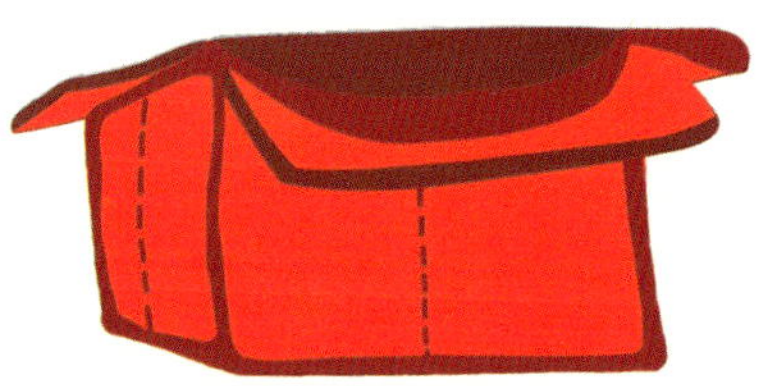

盒 hap2

boy

男孩 naam4 haai4

bracelet

手鏈 sau2 lin2

brain

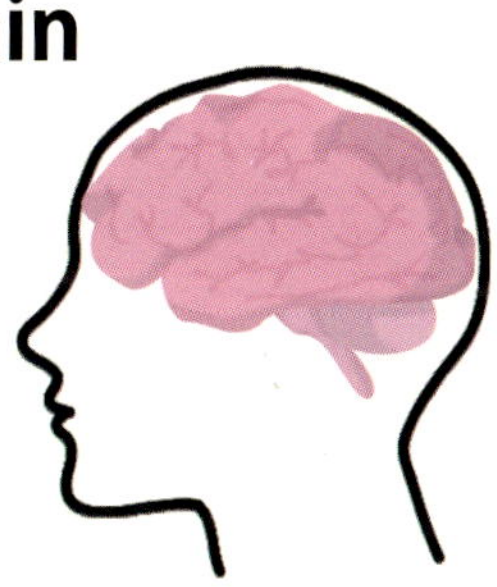

腦袋 nou5 doi6

branch

樹枝 syu6 zi1

bread

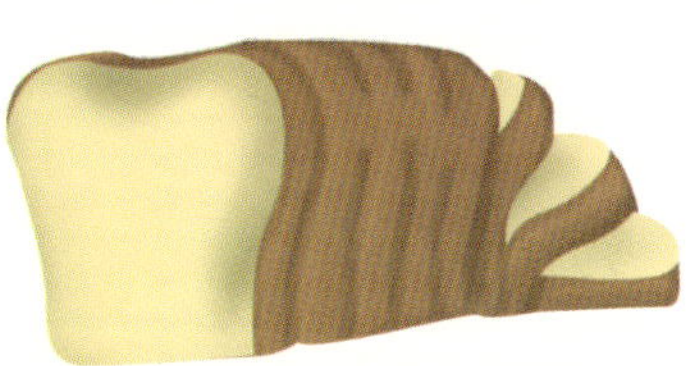

麪包 min6 baau1

breakfast

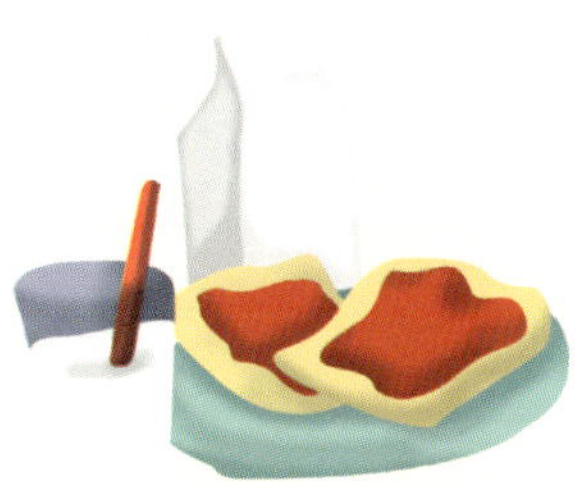

早餐 zou2 caan1

brick

磚頭 zyun1 tau4

a b c d e f g h i j k l m n o p q r s t u v w x y z

a b c d e f g h i j k l m n o p q r s t u v w x y z

bride

新娘 san^{1} noeng^{4}

bridegroom

新郎 san^{1} long^{4}

bridge

橋 kiu^{4}

broom

掃把 sou^{3} baa^{2}

brother

兄弟 hing^{1} dai^{6}

brown

啡色 fe^{1} sik^{1}

brush

刷 caat^{3}

bubble

泡沫 pou^{5} mut^{6}

bucket

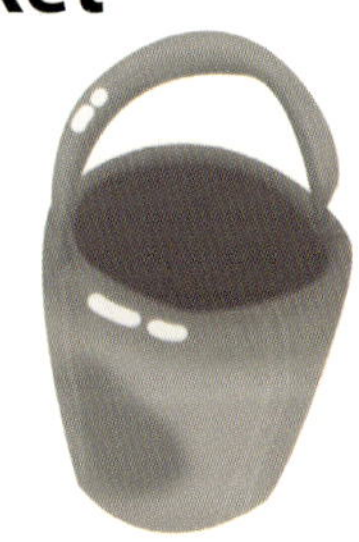

水桶 seoi^{2} tung^{2}

buffalo

公牛 gung^{1} ngau^{4}

building

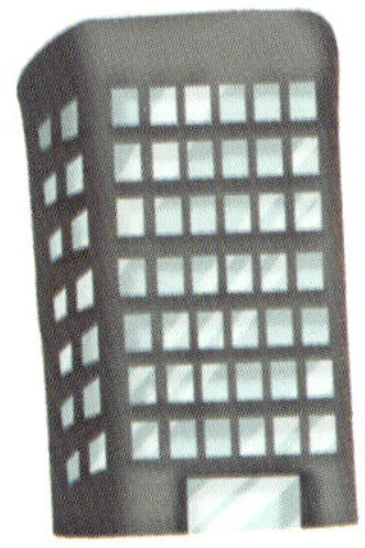

建築 gin^{3} zuk^{1}

bulb

燈膽 dang^{1} daam^{2}

bull

水牛 seoi^2 ngau^4

bun

麪包 min^6 baau^1

bunch

花束 faa^1 cuk^1

bundle

紮 zaat^3

bungalow

平房 ping^4 fong^4

burger

漢堡包 hon^3 bou^2 baau^1

bus

巴士 baa^1 si^2

bush

草叢 cou^2 cung^4

butcher

肉販 juk^6 faan^2

butter

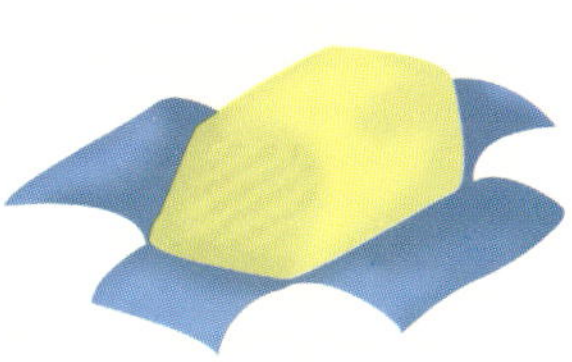

牛油 ngau^4 jau^4

butterfly

蝴蝶 wu^4 dip^6

button

鈕 nau^2

a b c d e f g h i j k l m n o p q r s t u v w x y z

Cc

cabbage

椰菜 je^4 coi^3

cabinet

櫃 gwai^6

cable

電線 din^6 sin^3

cable car

纜車 laam^6 ce^1

cactus

仙人掌
sin^1 jan^4 zoeng^2

cafe

咖啡店 gaa^3 fe^1 dim^3

cage

籠 lung^4

cake

蛋糕 daan^6 gou^1

calculator

計算機
gai^3 syun^3 gei^1

calendar

月曆 jyut^6 lik^6

calf

小牛 siu^2 ngau^4

camel

駱駝 lok^{3} to^{4}

camera

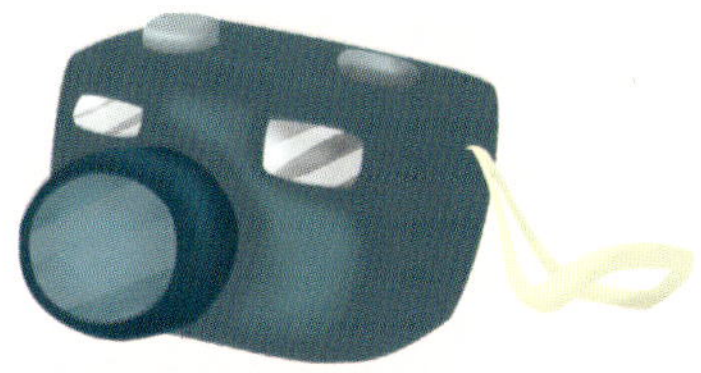

相機 soeng^{2} gei^{1}

camp

露營 lou^{6} jing^{4}

can

罐 gun^{3}

canal

運河 wan^{6} ho^{4}

candle

蠟燭 laap^{6} zuk^{1}

canoe

獨木舟
duk^{6} muk^{6} zau^{1}

canteen

飯堂 faan^{6} tong^{4}

cap

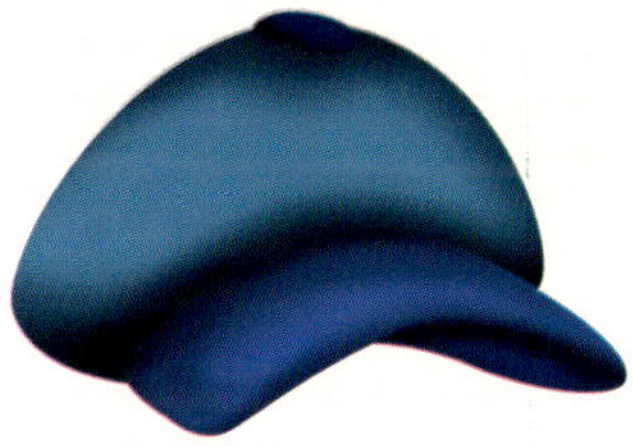

帽 mou^{2}

captain

船長 syun^{4} zoeng^{2}

car

汽車 hei^{3} ce^{1}

caravan

露營車 lou^{6} jing^{4} ce^{1}

card

卡 kaat^1

carnival

嘉年華 gaa^1 nin^4 waa^4

carpenter

木匠 muk^6 zoeng^6

carpet

地氈 dei^6 zin^1

carrot

蘿蔔 lo^4 baak^6

cart

手推車 sau^2 teoi^1 ce^1

cartoon

卡通 kaa^1 tung^1

cascade

瀑布 buk^6 bou^3

castle

城堡 sing^4 bou^2

cat

貓 maau^1

caterpillar

毛蟲 mou^4 cung^4

cauliflower

椰菜花 je^4 coi^3 faa^1

cave

洞穴 dung6 jyut6

ceiling

天花板 tin1 faa1 baan2

centipede

蜈蚣 ng4 gung1

centre

US English **center**

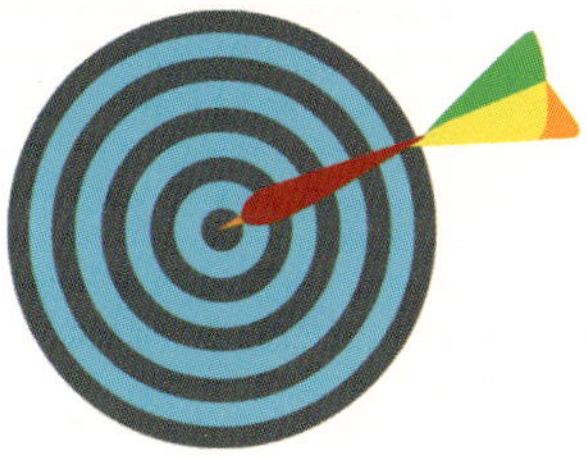

中心 zung1 sam1

cereal

穀物 guk1 mat6

chain

鏈 lin2

chair

椅 ji2

chalk

粉筆 fan2 bat1

cheek

面頰 min6 haap3

cheese

芝士 zi1 si2

chef

大廚 daai6 cyu2

cherry

車厘子 ce1 lei4 zi2

a b c d e f g h i j k l m n o p q r s t u v w x y z

a b **c** d e f g h i j k l m n o p q r s t u v w x y z

chess

棋 kei^2

chest

胸口 hung^1 hau^2

chick

小雞 siu^2 gai^1

chilli

US English **chili**

辣椒 laat^6 ziu^1

chimney

煙囪 jin^1 tung^1

chin

下巴 haa^6 baa^1

chocolate

朱古力
zyu^1 gu^2 lik^6

Christmas

聖誕節
sing^3 daan^3 zit^3

church

教堂 gaau^3 tong^4

cinema

戲院 hei^3 jyun^2

circle

圓 jyun^4

circus

馬戲團
maa^5 hei^3 tyun^4

city

城市 sing^4 si^5

classroom

課室 fo^3 sat^1

clinic

診所 can^2 so^2

clock

時鐘 si^4 zung^1

cloth
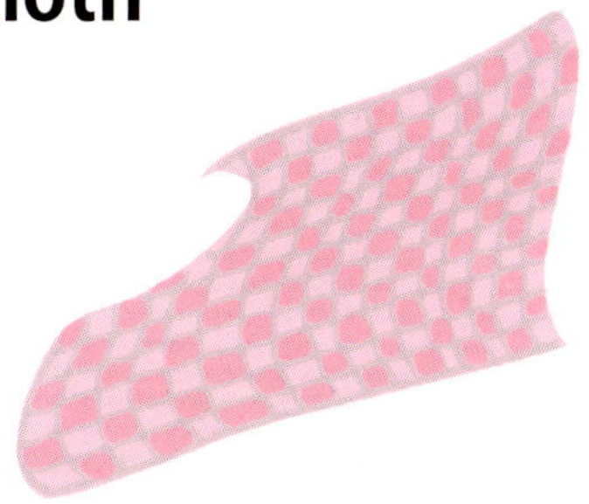

布 bou^3

cloud

雲 wan^4

clown

小丑 siu^2 cau^2

coal

煤 mui^4

coast

海岸 hoi^2 ngon^6

coat

大褸 daai^6 lau^1

cobra

眼鏡蛇
ngaan^5 geng^3 se^4

cockerel
US English **rooster**

公雞 gung^1 gai^1

cockroach

甲由 gaat^{6} zaat^{2}

coconut

椰子 je^{4} zi^{2}

coffee

咖啡 gaa^{3} fe^{1}

coin

硬幣 ngaang^{6} bai^{6}

colour
US English **color**

顏色 ngaan^{4} sik^{1}

comb

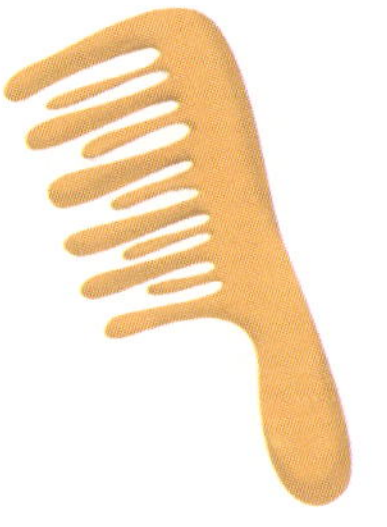

梳 so^{1}

comet

彗星 seoi^{6} sing^{1}

compass

指南針
zi^{2} naam^{4} zam^{1}

computer

電腦 din^{6} nou^{5}

cone

雪糕筒
syut^{3} gou^{1} tung^{2}

container

容器 jung^{4} hei^{3}

cook

廚師 cyu^{4} si^{1}

cookie

曲奇 kuk1 kei4

cord

電線 din6 sin3

corn

粟米 suk1 mai5

cot

嬰兒床 jing1 ji4 cong4

cottage

農舍 nung4 se3

cotton

棉 min4

country

國家 gwok3 gaa1

couple

情侶 cing4 leoi5

court

法庭 faat3 ting4

cow

牛 ngau4

crab

蟹 haai5

crane

起重機 hei2 cung5 gei1

crayon

蠟筆 laap6 bat1

crocodile

鱷魚 ngok6 jyu4

cross

十字架 sap6 zi6 gaa3

crow

烏鴉 wu1 aa1

crowd

人群 jan4 kwan4

crown

皇冠 wong4 gun1

cube

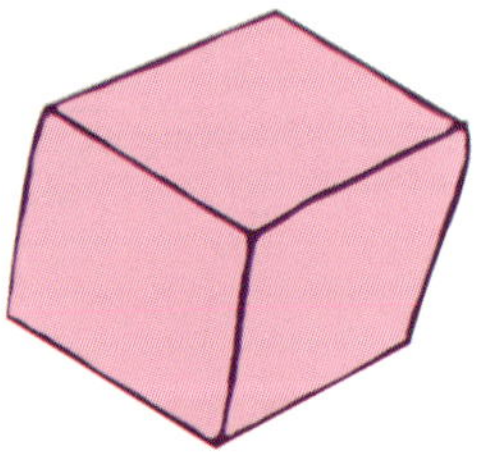

立方體 lap6 fong1 tai2

cucumber

青瓜 ceng1 gwaa1

cup

杯 bui1

cupboard

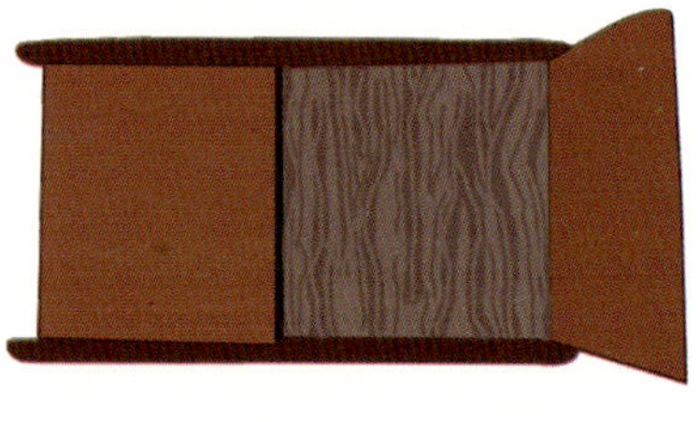

櫃 guai6

curtain

窗簾 coeng1 lim2

cushion

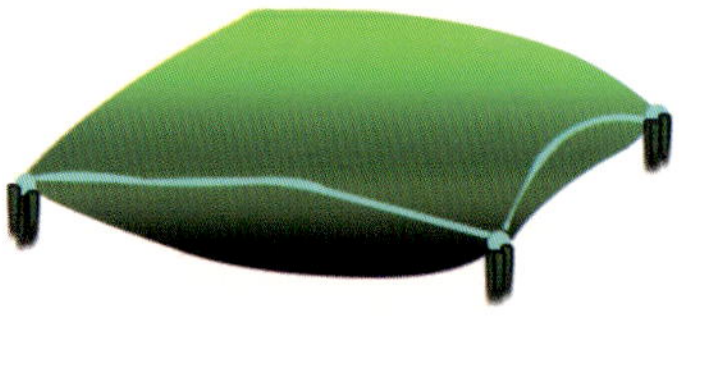

咕臣 gu1 seon2

Dd

dam

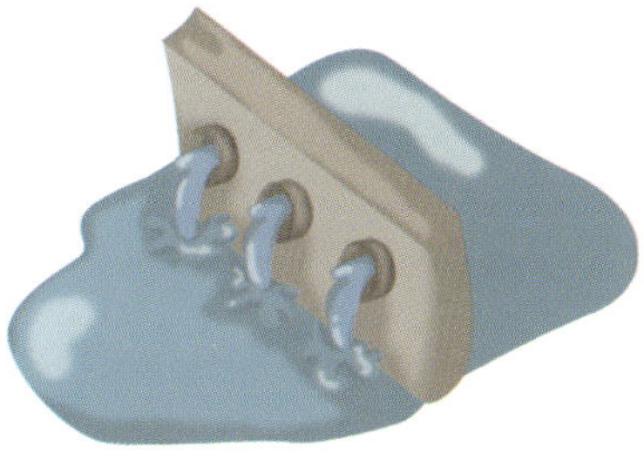

水壩 seoi2 baa3

dancer

舞蹈員 mou5 dou6 jyun4

dart

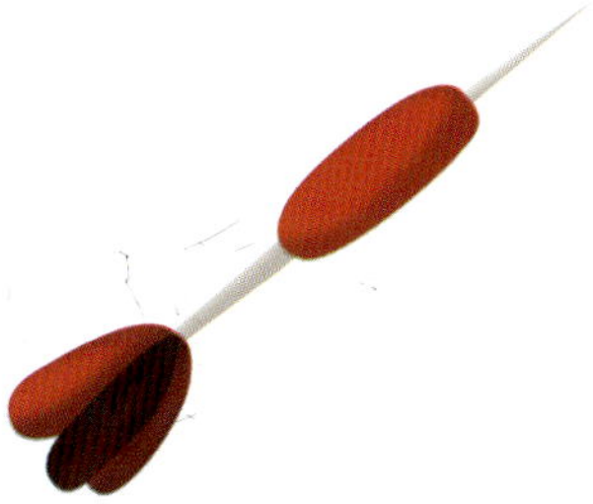

飛鏢 fei1 biu1

data

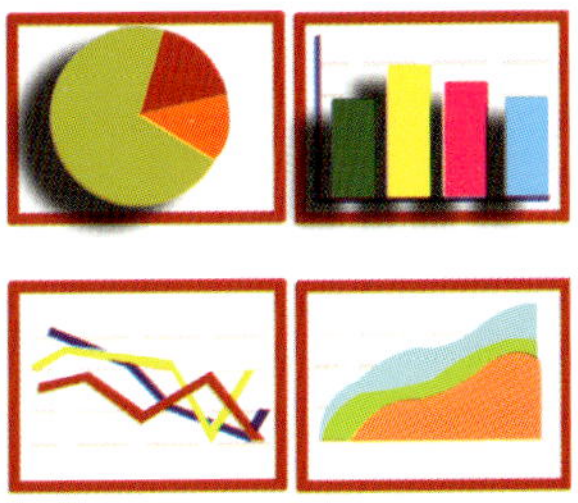

數據 sou3 geoi3

dates

棗 zou2

daughter

女兒 neoi5 ji4

day

白天 baak6 tin1

deck

啤牌 pe1 paai2

deer

鹿 luk6

den

巢穴 caau4 jyut6

dentist

牙醫 ngaa4 ji1

desert

沙漠 saa^1 mok^6

design

設計 cit^3 gai^3

desk

桌子 coek^3 zi^2

dessert

甜品 tim^4 ban^2

detective

偵探 zing^1 taam^3

diamond

鑽石 zyun^3 sek^6

diary

日記 jat^6 gei^3

dice

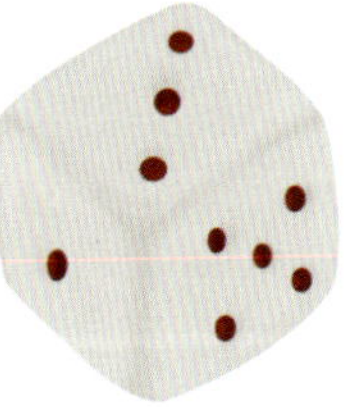

骰 sik^1

dictionary

字典 zi^6 din^2

dinosaur

恐龍 hung^2 lung^4

disc

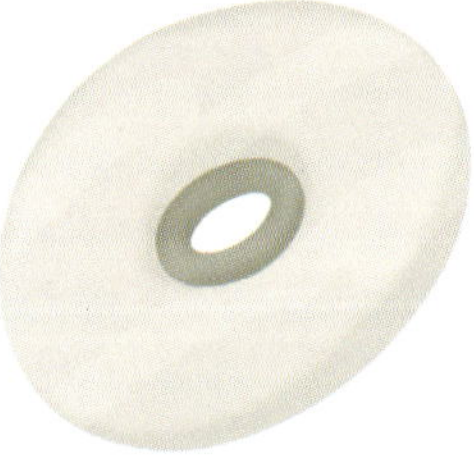

鐳射唱片
leoi^4 se^6 coeng^3 pin^2

dish

碟 dip^6

diver

潛水員
cim4 seoi2 jyun4

dock

船塢 syun4 wu2

doctor

醫生 ji1 saang1

dog

狗 gau2

doll

洋娃娃
joeng4 waa1 waa1

dolphin

海豚 hoi2 tyun4

dome

圓頂 jyun4 deng2

domino

骨牌 gwat1 paai4

donkey

驢 lou4

donut

冬甩 dung1 lat1

door

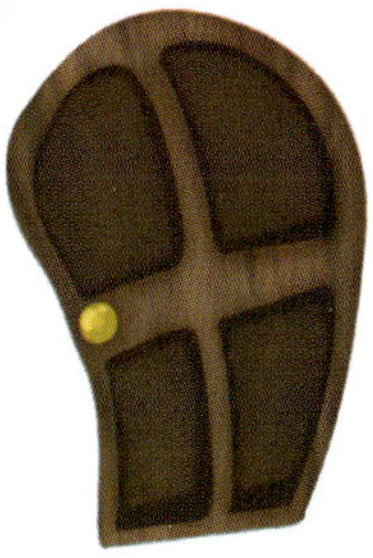

門 mun4

dough

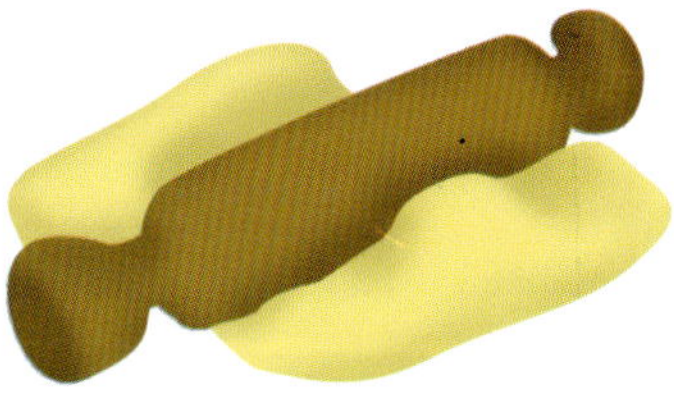

麪團 min6 tyun4

a b c d e f g h i j k l m n o p q r s t u v w x y z

dragon

龍 lung^{4}

drain

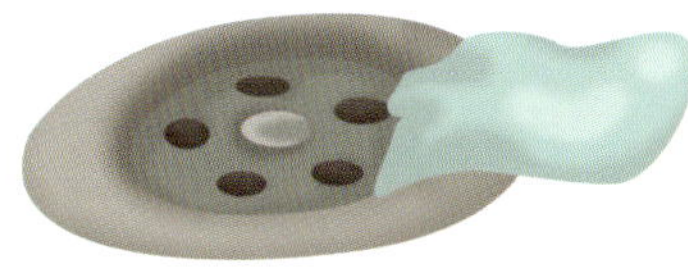

排水口 paai^{4} seoi^{2} hau^{2}

drawer

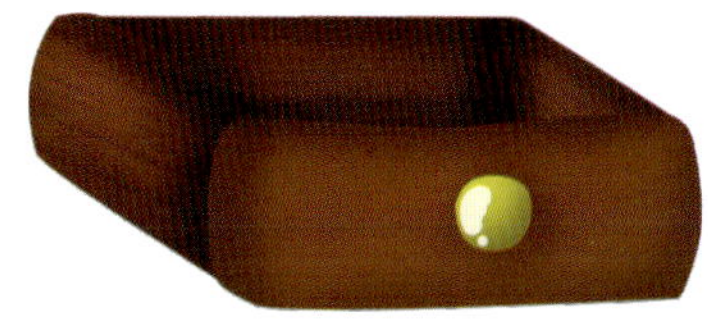

抽屜 cau^{1} tai^{3}

drawing

畫畫 waak^{6} waa^{2}

dream

夢 mung^{6}

dress

裙 kwan^{4}

drink

飲品 jam^{2} ban^{2}

driver

司機 si^{1} gei^{1}

drop

水滴 seoi^{2} dik^{6}

drought

乾旱 gon^{1} hon^{5}

drum

鼓 gu^{2}

duck

鴨 ngaap^{3}

dustbin
US English **trash can**

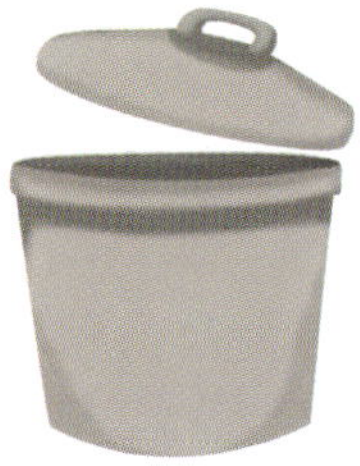

垃圾桶
laap6 saap3 tung2

duvet

羽絨被
jyu5 jung2 pei5

dwarf

小矮人
siu2 ngai2 jan4

Ee

eagle

鷹 jing1

ear

耳 ji5

earring

耳環 ji5 waan2

earth

地球 dei6 kau4

earthquake

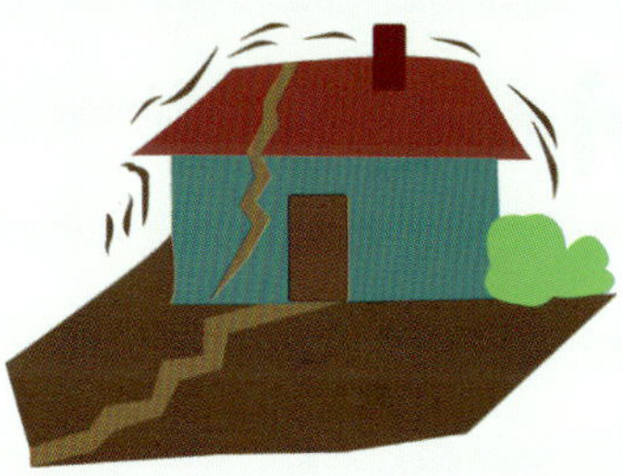

地震 dei6 zan3

earthworm

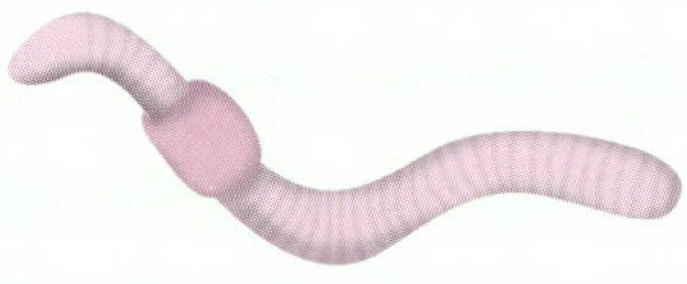

蚯蚓 jau1 jan5

eclipse

日食 jat6 sik6

edge

邊沿 bin1 jyun4

eel

鰻魚 maan6 jyu4

egg

蛋 daan2

eight

八 baat3

elastic

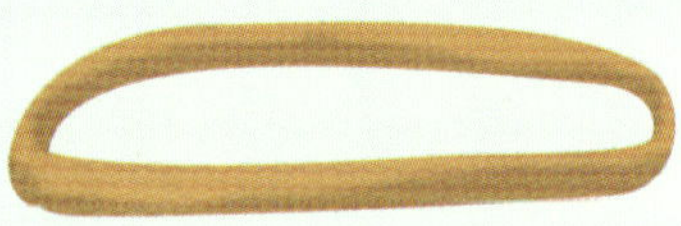

橡筋 zoeng6 gan1

elbow

手肘 sau2 zaau2

electrician

電工 din6 gung1

electricity

電力 din6 lik6

elephant

大象 daai6 zoeng6

elevator

升降機 sing1 gong3 gei1

elf

精靈 zing1 ling4

email

電郵 din6 jau4

embroidery

刺繡 ci3 sau3

engine

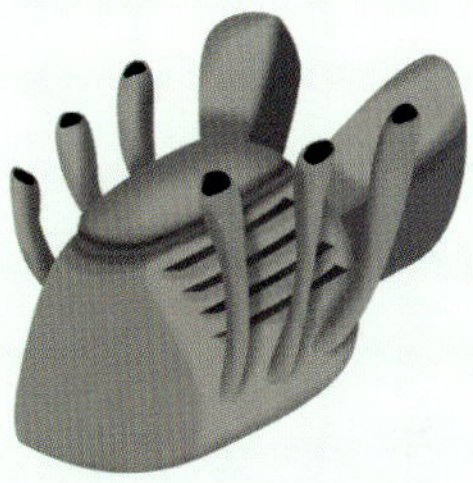

引擎 jan^5 king^4

entrance

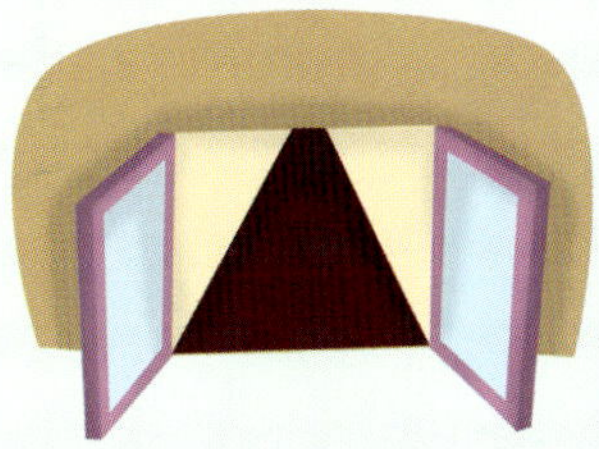

入口 jap^6 hau^2

envelope

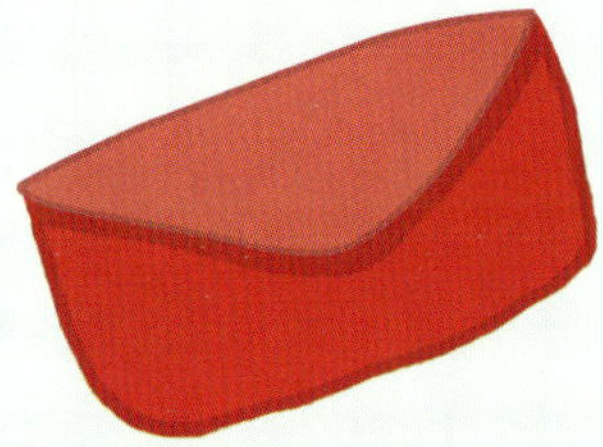

信封 seon^3 fung^1

equator

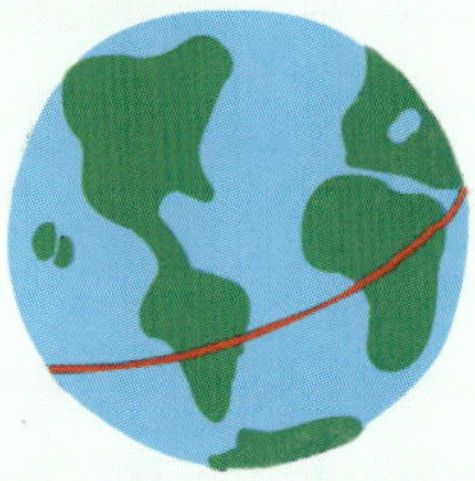

赤道 cek^3 dou^6

equipment

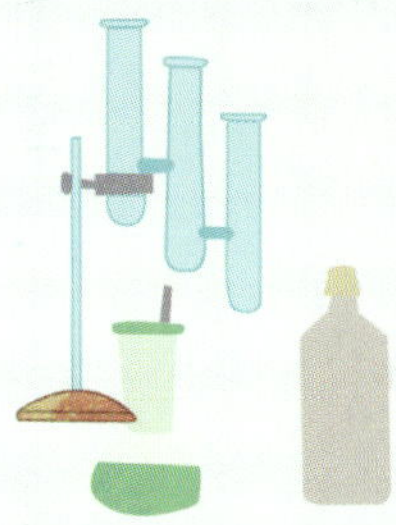

設備 cit^3 bei^6

eraser

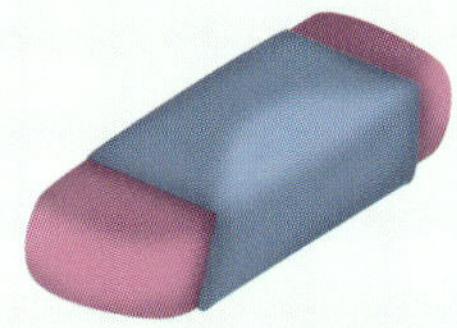

擦膠 caat^3 gaau^1

escalator

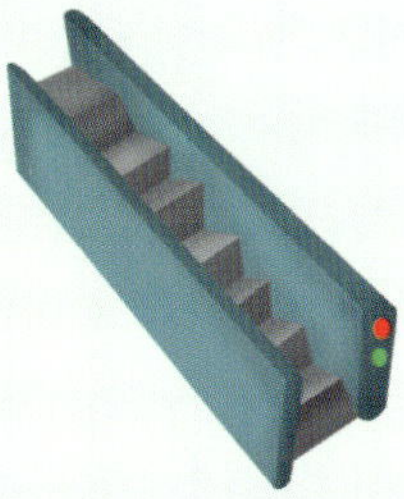

扶手電梯
fu^4 sau^2 din^6 tai^1

eskimo

愛斯基摩人
ngoi^3 si^1 gei^1 mo^1 jan^4

evening

黃昏 wong^4 fan^1

exhibition

展覽 zin^2 laam^5

eye

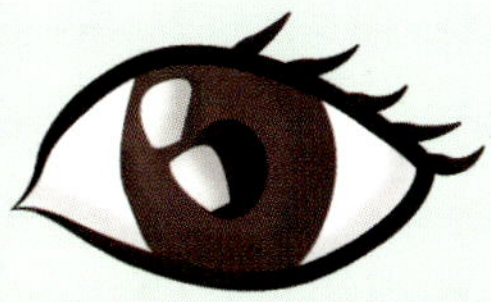

眼睛 ngaan^5 zing^1

eyebrow

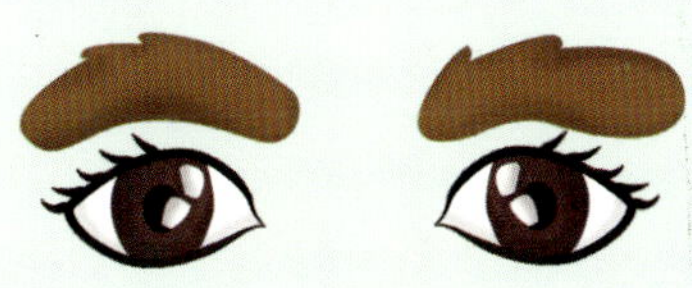

眼眉 ngaan^5 mei^4

a b c d e f g h i j k l m n o p q r s t u v w x y z

Ff

fabric

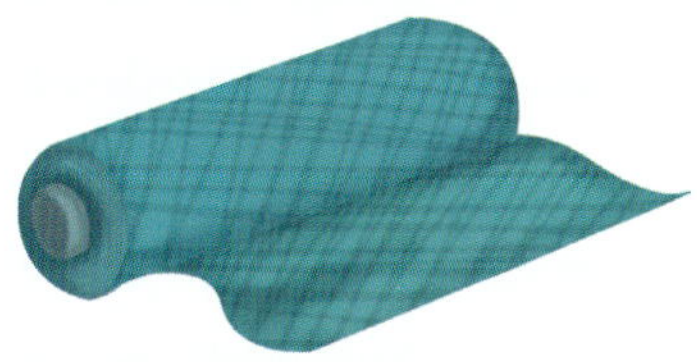

布料 bou^{3} liu^{2}

face

臉 lim^{5}

factory

工廠 gung^{1} cong^{2}

fairy

仙女 sin^{1} neoi^{5}

family

家庭 gaa^{1} ting^{4}

fan

風扇 fung^{1} sin^{3}

farm

農場 nung^{4} coeng^{4}

farmer

農夫 nung^{4} fu^{1}

fat

肥胖 fei^{4} bun^{6}

father

爸爸 baa^{1} baa^{1}

feather

羽毛 jyu^{5} mou^{4}

female

女性 neoi5 sing3

fence

圍欄 wai4 laan4

ferry

渡輪 dou6 leon4

field

田 tin4

fig

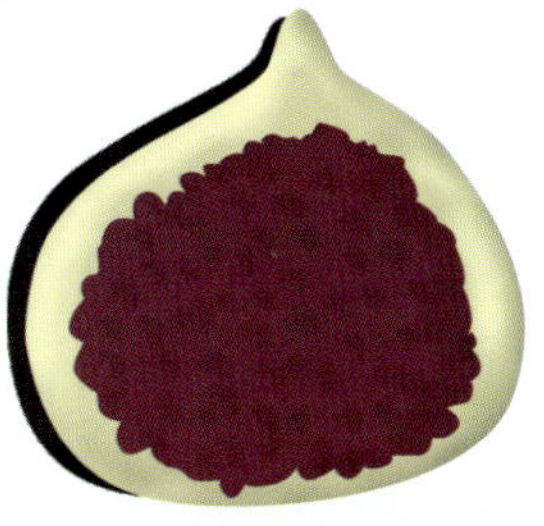

無花果
mou4 faa1 gwo2

file

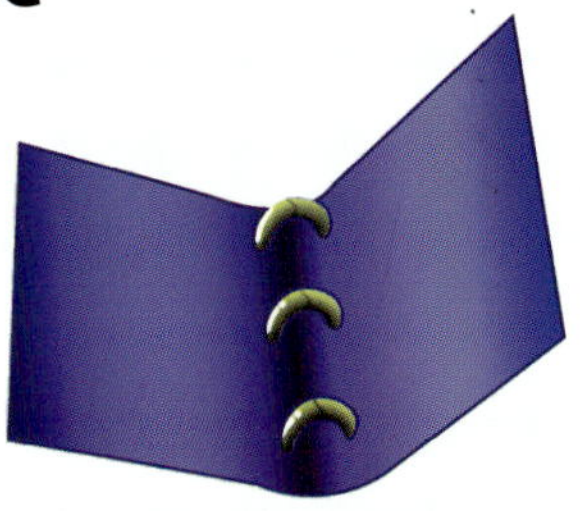

文件夾
man4 gin2 gaap3

film

電影 din6 jing2

finger

手指 sau2 zi2

fire

火 fo2

fire engine

消防車
siu1 fong4 ce1

fire fighter

消防員
siu1 fong4 jyun4

fireworks

煙花 jin1 faa1

fish

魚 jyu^2

fist

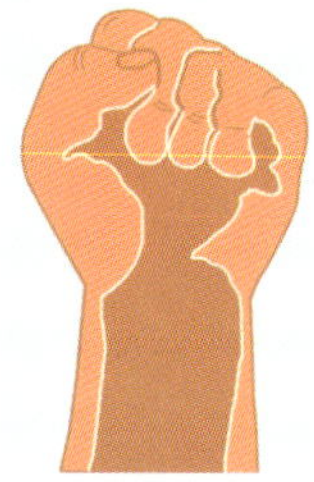

拳頭 kyun^4 tau^4

five

五 ng^5

flag

旗 kei^4

flame

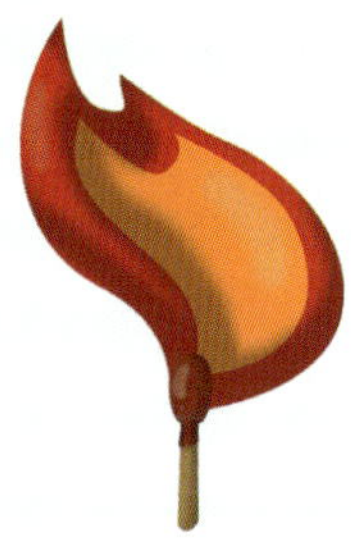

火焰 fo^2 jim^6

flamingo

紅鶴 hung^4 hok^6

flask

保溫杯 bou^2 wan^1 bui^1

flock

羊群 joeng^4 kwan^4

flood

水浸 seoi^2 zam^3

floor

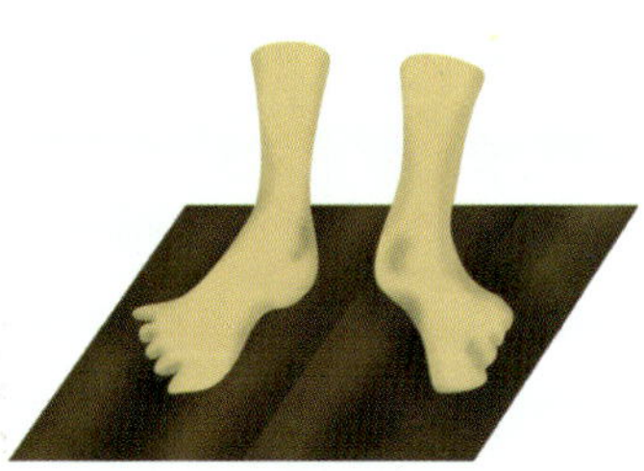

地板 dei^6 baan^2

florist

花店店員 faa^1 dim^3 dim^3 jyun^4

flour

麵粉 min^6 fan^2

flower

花 faa1

flute

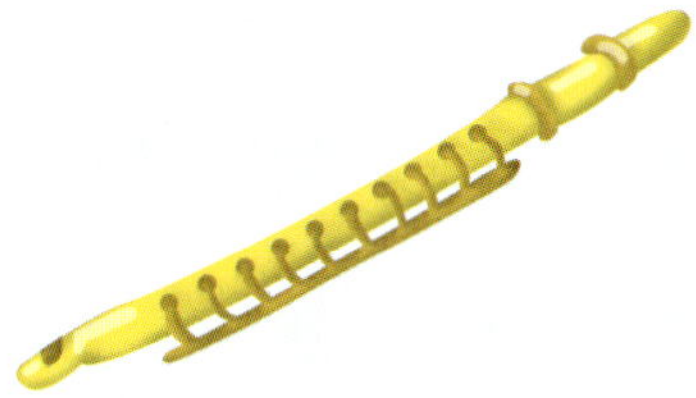

長笛 coeng4 dek2

fly

烏蠅 wu1 jing1

foam

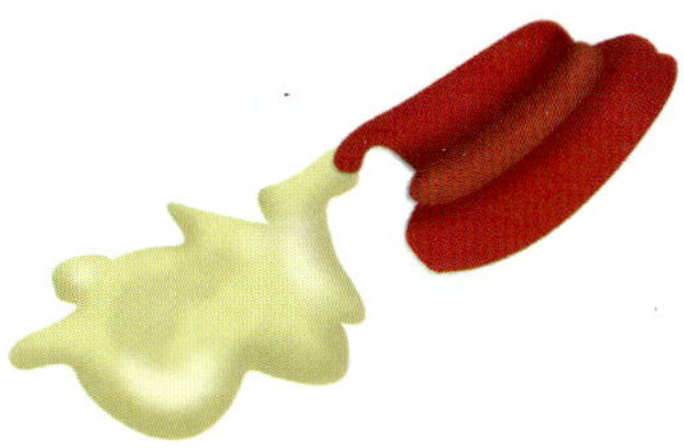

泡沫 pou5 mut6

fog

霧 mou6

foil

錫紙 sek3 zi2

food

食物 sik6 mat6

foot

腳 goek3

football
US English **soccer**

足球 zuk1 kau4

forearm

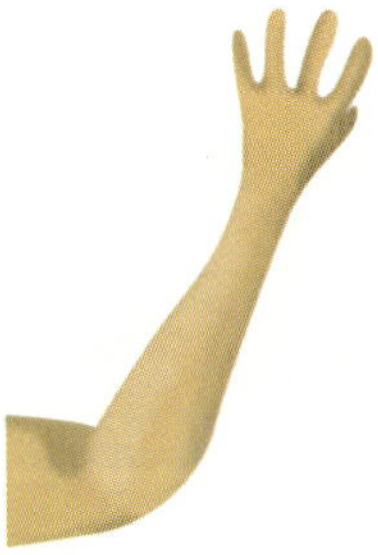

前臂 cin4 bei3

forehead

額頭 ngaak6 tau4

forest

樹林 syu6 lam4

a b c d e f g h i j k l m n o p q r s t u v w x y z

fork

叉 caa1

fortress

堡壘 bou2 leoi5

fountain

噴泉 pan3 cyun4

four

四 sei3

fox

狐狸 wui4 lei2

frame

相架 soeng2 gaa2

freezer

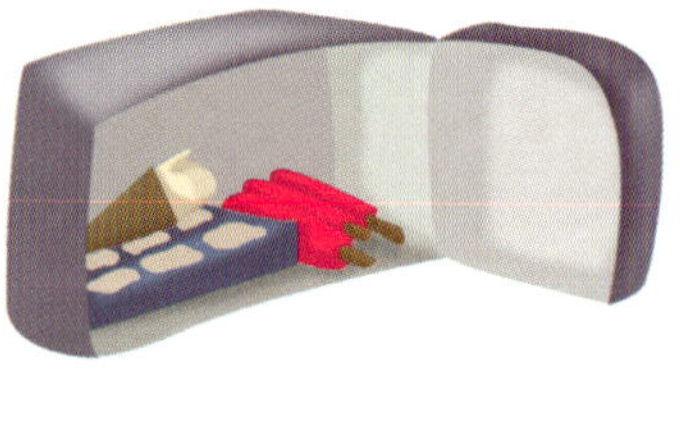

冰箱 bing1 soeng1

fridge
US English **refrigerator**

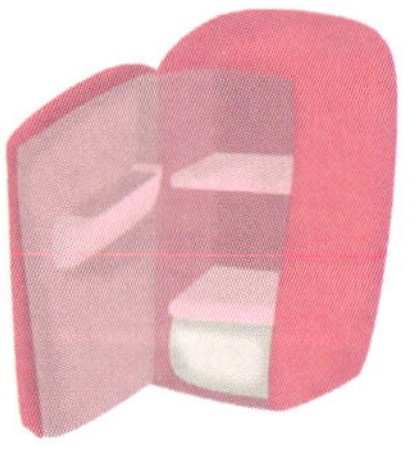

雪櫃 syut3 gwai6

friend

朋友 pang4 jau5

frog

青蛙 cing1 waa1

fruit

水果 seoi2 gwo2

fumes

煙霧 jin1 mou6

funnel

漏斗 lau⁶ dau²

furnace

火爐 fo² lou⁴

furniture

傢俬 gaa¹ si¹

Gg

gadget

小工具
siu² gung¹ geoi⁶

gallery

畫廊 waa² long⁴

game

遊戲 jau⁴ hei³

gap

空隙 hung¹ gwik¹

garage

停車場
ting⁴ ce¹ coeng⁴

garbage

垃圾 laap⁶ saap³

garden

花園 faa¹ jyun²

garland

花圈 faa¹ hyun¹

garlic

大蒜 daai^{6} syun^{3}

gas

石油氣 sek^{6} jau^{4} hei^{3}

gate

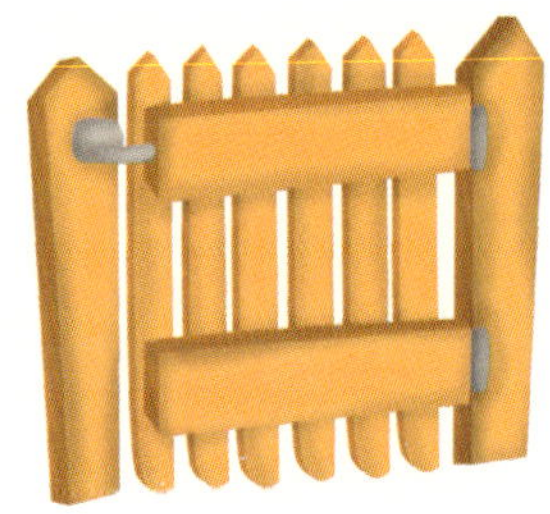

閘門 zaap^{6} mun^{4}

gem

寶石 bou^{2} sek^{6}

generator

發電機 faat^{3} din^{6} gei^{1}

germ

細菌 sai^{3} kwan^{2}

geyser

間歇泉 gaan^{3} hit^{3} cyun^{4}

ghost

鬼 gwai^{2}

giant

巨人 geoi^{6} jan^{4}

gift

禮物 lai^{5} mat^{6}

ginger

薑 goeng^{1}

giraffe

長頸鹿 coeng^{4} geng^{2} luk^{2}

girl

女孩 neoi⁵ haai⁴

glacier

冰川 bing¹ cyun¹

glass

玻璃 bo¹ lei¹

glider

滑翔翼
waat⁶ coeng⁴ jik⁶

globe

全球 cyun⁴ kau⁴

glove
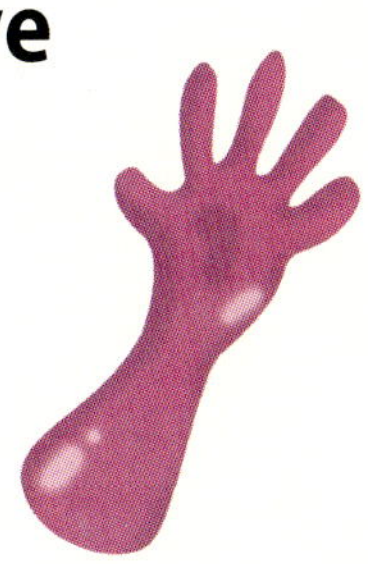
手套 sau² tou³

glue
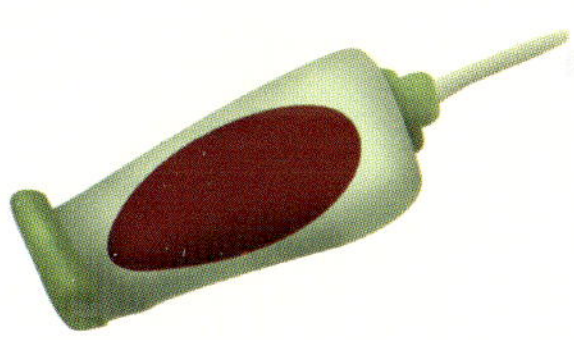
膠水 gaau¹ seoi²

goal
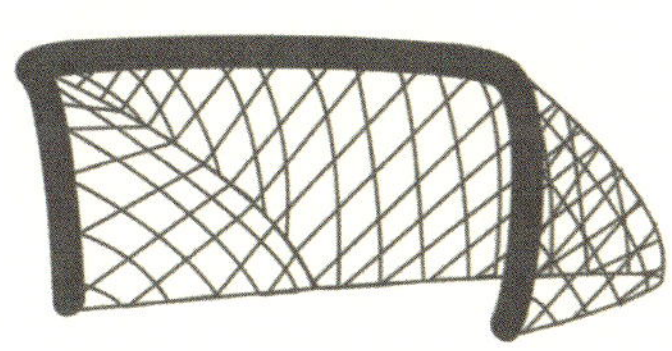
龍門 lung⁴ mun⁴

goat

山羊 saan¹ joeng⁴

gold

金 gam¹

golf

高爾夫球
gou¹ ji⁵ fu¹ kau⁴

goose

鵝 ngo⁴

a b c d e f g h i j k l m n o p q r s t u v w x y z

gorilla

大猩猩
daai^6 sing^1 sing^1

grain

穀物 guk^1 mat^6

grandfather

爺爺 / 公公
je^4 je^2 / gung^1 gung^1

grandmother

嫲嫲 / 婆婆
maa^4 maa^4 / po^4 po^1

grape

提子 tai^4 zi^2

grapefruit

西柚 sai^1 jau^2

grass

草 cou^2

grasshopper

草蜢 cou^2 maang^5

gravel

沙礫 saa^1 lik^1

green

綠色 luk^6 sik^1

grey

灰色 fui^1 sik^1

grill

燒烤 siu^1 haau^1

grocery

食品 sik⁶ ban²

ground

地 dei⁶

guard

保安 bou² ngon¹

guava

番石榴
faan¹ sek⁶ lau²

guide

導遊 dou⁶ jau⁴

guitar

吉他 gat¹ taa¹

gulf

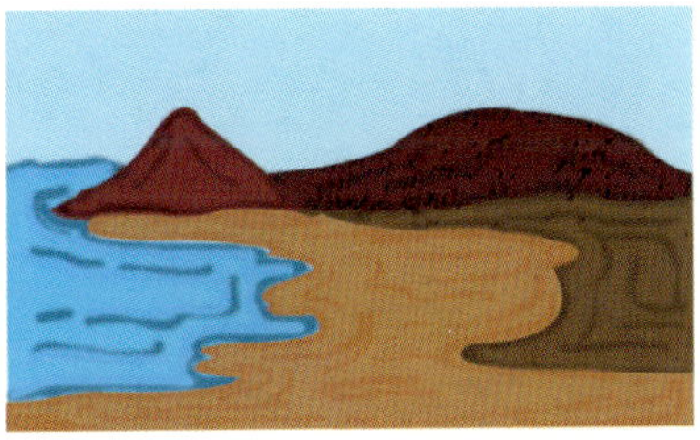

海灣 hoi² waan¹

gun

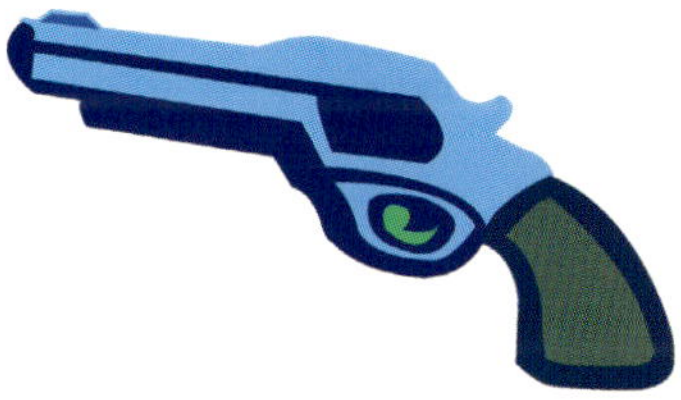

槍 coeng¹

gypsy

吉卜賽人
gat¹ buk¹ coi³ jan⁴

Hh

hair

頭髮 tau⁴ faat³

hairbrush

梳 so¹

hairdresser

髮型師
faat^{3} jing^{4} si^{1}

half
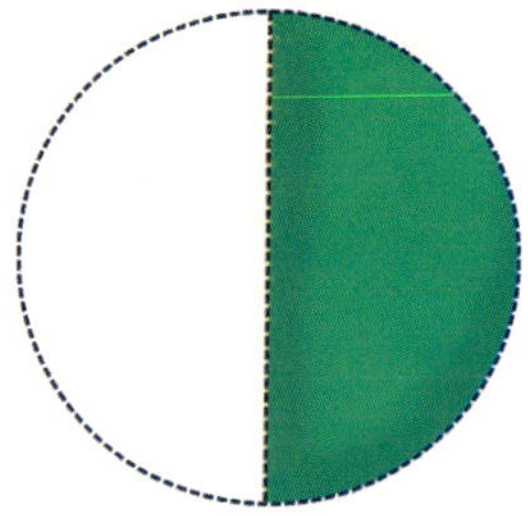
一半 jat^{1} bun^{3}

hall

禮堂 lai^{5} tong^{4}

ham

火腿 fo^{2} teoi^{2}

hammer

錘仔 ceoi^{4} zai^{2}

hammock

吊床 diu^{3} cong^{4}

hand
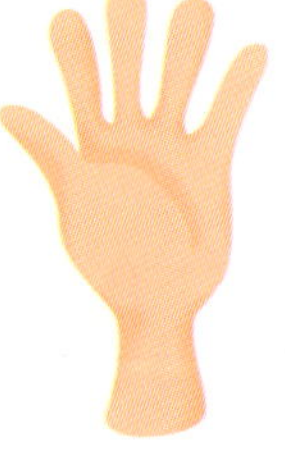
手 sau^{2}

handbag

手袋 sau^{2} doi^{2}

handicraft

手工藝
sau^{2} gung^{1} ngai^{6}

handkerchief

手巾 sau^{2} gan^{1}

handle
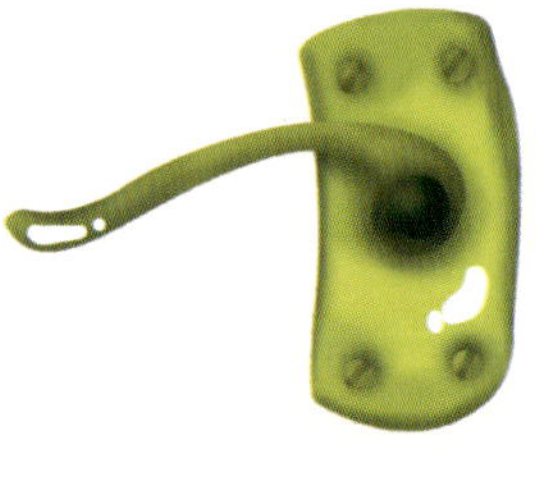
手把 sau^{2} baa^{2}

hanger

衣架 ji^{1} gaa^{2}

harbour
US English **harbor**

海港 hoi2 gong2

hare

野兔 je5 tou3

harvest

收成 sau1 sing4

hat

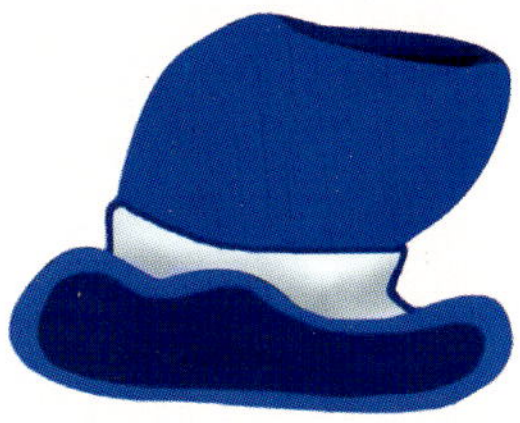

帽 mou6

hawk

鷹 jing1

hay

稻草 dou6 cou2

head

頭 tau4

headphone

耳機 ji5 gei1

heap

一堆 jat1 deoi1

heart

心 sam1

heater

暖爐 nyun5 lou4

hedge

樹籬 syu6 lei4

heel

高踭鞋
gou1 zaang1 haai4

helicopter

直升機
zik6 sing1 gei1

helmet

頭盔 tau4 kwai1

hen

母雞 mou5 gai1

herb

草本植物
cou2 bun2 zik6 mat6

herd

一群 jat1 kwan4

hermit

隱士 jan2 si6

hill

山丘 saan1 jau1

hippopotamus

河馬 ho4 maa5

hive

蜂巢 fung1 caau4

hole
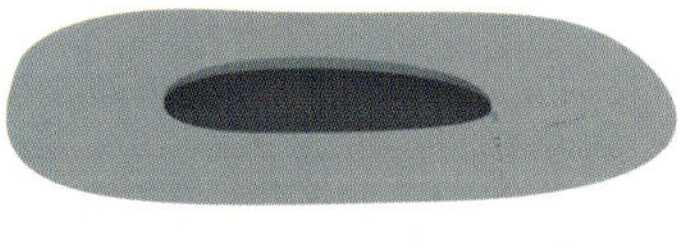
洞 dung6

honey

蜜糖 mat6 tong4

hood

兜帽 dau^{1} mou^{2}

hook

鈎 ngau^{1}

horn

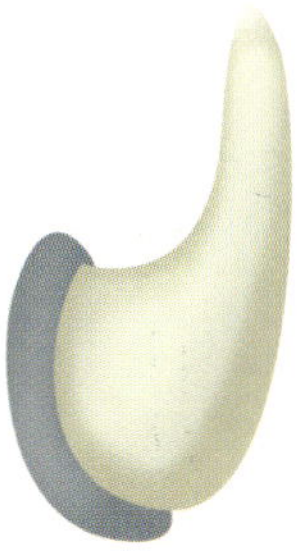

角 gok^{3}

horse

馬 maa^{5}

hose

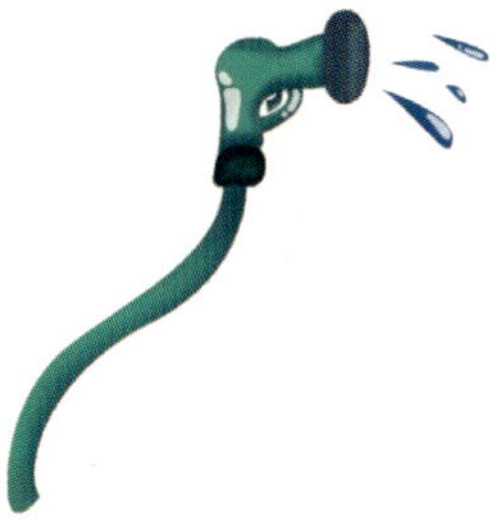

水喉 seoi^{2} hau^{4}

hospital

醫院 ji^{1} jyun^{2}

hotdog

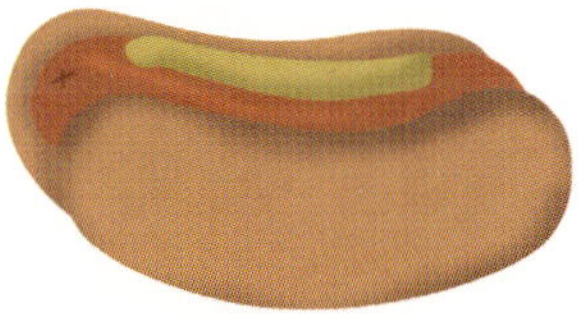

熱狗 jit^{6} gau^{2}

hotel

酒店 zau^{2} dim^{3}

hour

小時 siu^{2} si^{4}

house

屋 nguk^{1}

human

人類 jan^{4} leoi^{6}

hunter

獵人 lip^{6} jan^{4}

hurricane

龍捲風
lung⁴ gyun² fung¹

husband

丈夫 zoeng⁶ fu¹

hut

小屋 siu² nguk¹

Ii

ice

冰 bing¹

iceberg

冰山 bing¹ saan¹

ice cream

雪糕 syut³ gou¹

idol

偶像 ngau⁵ zoeng⁶

igloo

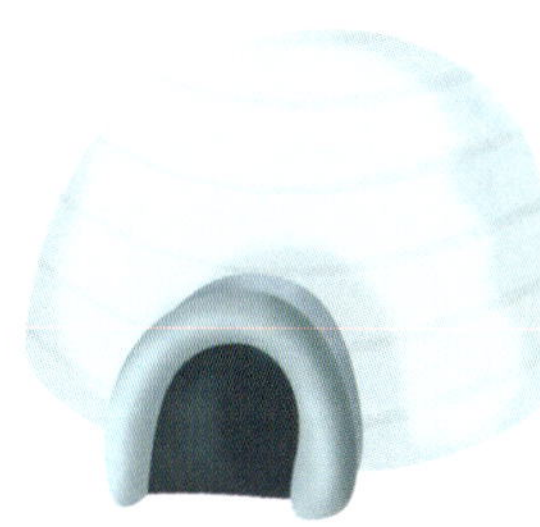

冰屋 bing¹ nguk¹

inch

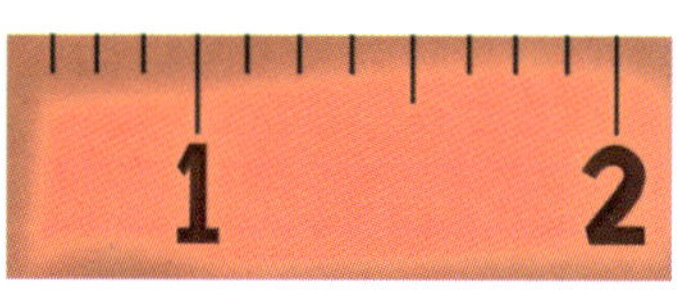

吋 cyun³

injection

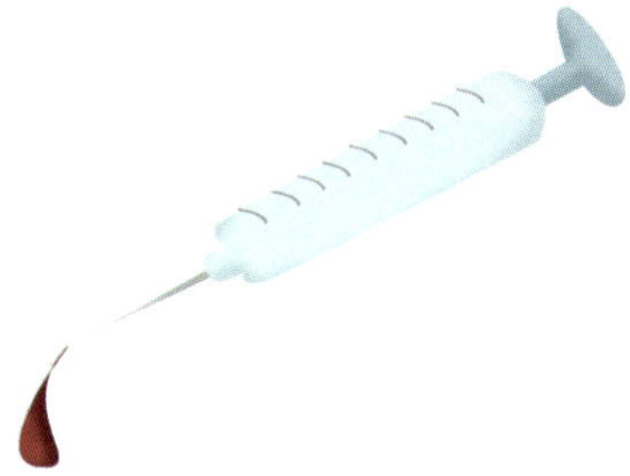

注射 zyu³ se⁶

injury

受傷 sau⁶ soeng¹

ink

墨 mak⁶

inn

旅店 leoi⁵ dim³

insect

昆蟲 kwan¹ cung⁴

inspector

檢查員
gim² caa⁴ jyun⁴

instrument

樂器 ngok⁶ hei³

internet

互聯網
wu⁶ lyun⁴ mong⁵

intestine

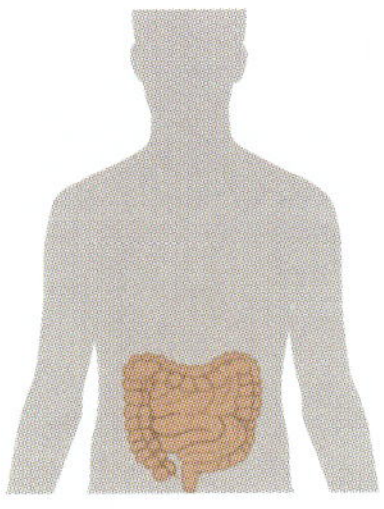

腸臟 coeng⁴ zong⁶

inventor

發明家
faat³ ming⁴ gaa¹

invitation

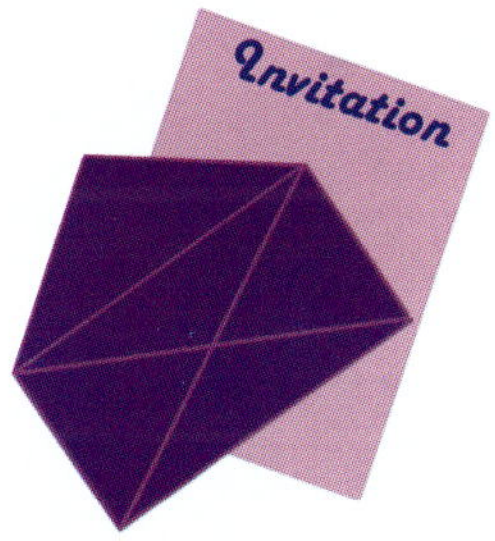

邀請 jiu¹ cing²

iron

熨斗 tong³ dau²

island

島 dou²

ivory

象牙 zoeng⁶ ngaa⁴

Jj

jackal

豺 caai^{4}

jacket

外套 ngoi^{6} tou^{3}

jackfruit

大樹菠蘿 daai^{6} syu^{6} bo^{1} lo^{4}

jam

果醬 gwo^{2} zoeng^{3}

jar

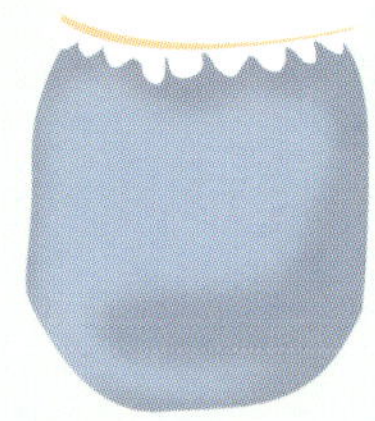

樽 zeon^{1}

javelin

標槍 biu^{1} coeng^{1}

jaw

下顎 haa^{6} ngok^{6}

jeans

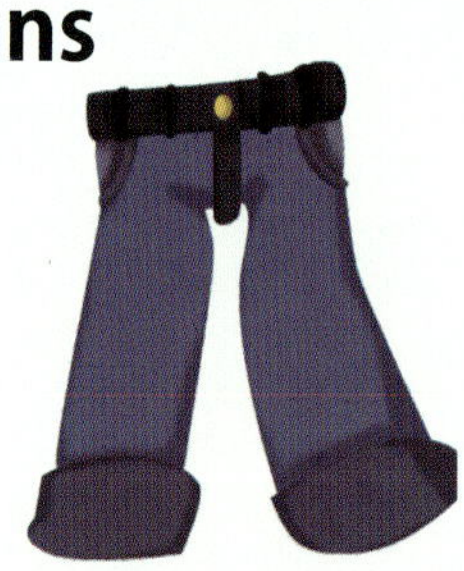

牛仔褲 ngau^{4} zai^{2} fu^{3}

jelly

啫喱 ze^{1} lei^{2}

jetty

碼頭 maa^{5} tau^{4}

jewellery

US English **jewelry**

首飾 sau^{2} sik^{1}

jigsaw

砌圖 cai^3 tou^4

jockey

騎師 ke^4 si^1

joker

小丑 siu^2 cau^2

journey

旅行 leoi^5 hang^4

jug

水壺 seoi^2 wu^2

juggler

雜技員 zaap^6 gei^6 jyun^4

juice

果汁 gwo^2 zap^1

jungle

森林 sam^1 lam^4

jute

黃麻 wong^4 maa^4

Kk

kangaroo

袋鼠 doi^6 syu^2

kennel

狗屋 gau^2 nguk^1

kerb
US English **curb**

石壘 sek⁶ bok³

kerosene

火水 fo² seoi²

ketchup

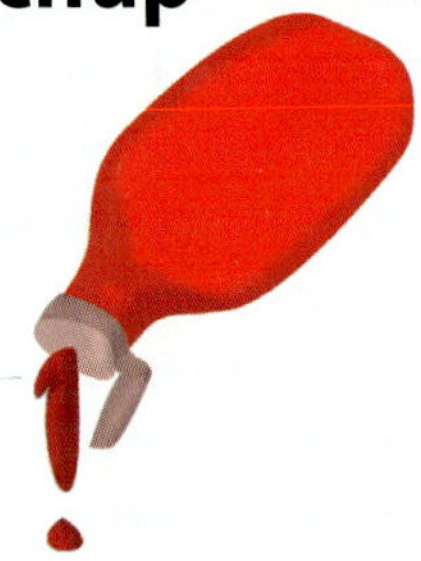

茄汁 ke² zap¹

kettle

水煲 seoi² bou¹

key

鎖匙 so² si⁴

keyboard

鍵盤 gin⁶ pun⁴

key ring

鎖匙圈 so² si⁴ hyun¹

kidney

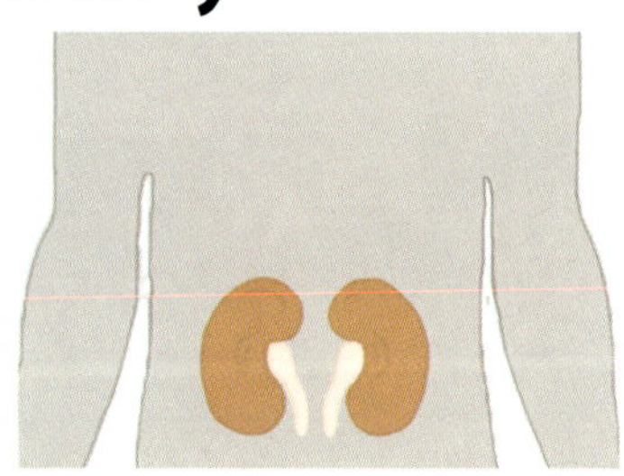

腎 san⁶

kilogram

公斤 gung¹ gan¹

king

國王 gwok³ wong⁴

kiosk

小食亭 siu² sik⁶ ting⁴

kiss

吻 man⁵

kitchen

廚房 cyu^{4} fong^{2}

kite

風箏 fung^{1} zaang^{1}

kitten

小貓 siu^{2} maau^{1}

kiwi

奇異果 kei^{4} ji^{6} gwo^{2}

knee

膝 sat^{1}

knife

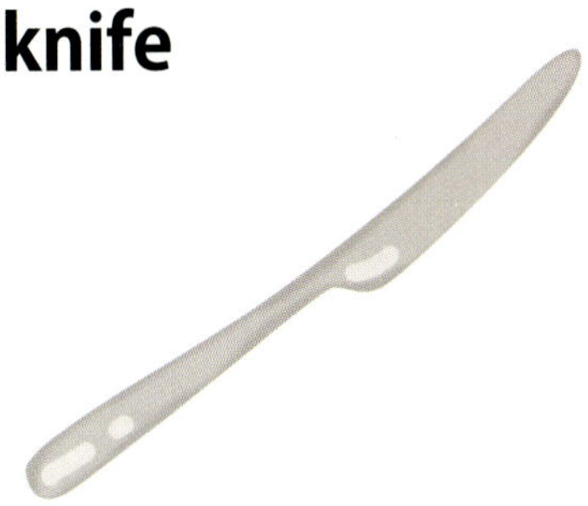

刀 dou^{1}

knight

騎士 ke^{4} si^{6}

knitwear

毛衣 mou^{4} ji^{1}

knob

門鎖 mun^{4} so^{2}

knock

敲 haau^{1}

knot

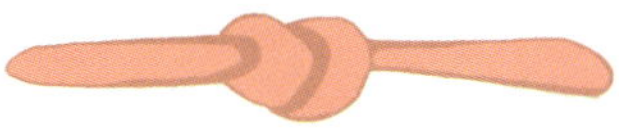

結 git^{3}

knuckle

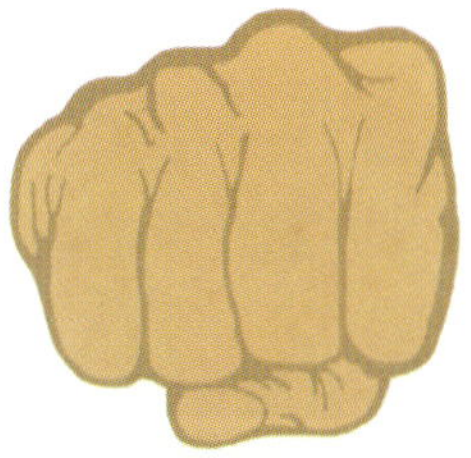

指關節 zi^{2} gwaan^{1} zit^{3}

Ll

label

標籤 biu¹ cim¹

laboratory

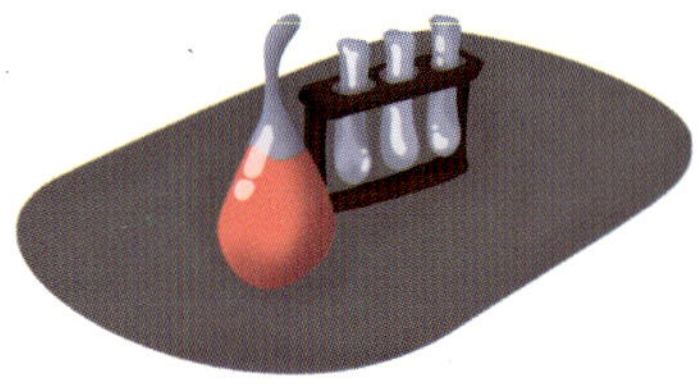

實驗室 sat⁶ jim⁶ sat¹

lace

鞋帶 haai⁴ daai²

ladder

梯 tai¹

lady

女士 neoi⁵ si⁶

ladybird
US English **ladybug**

瓢蟲 piu⁴ cung⁴

lagoon

潟湖 sik¹ wu⁴

lake

湖 wu⁴

lamb

小羊 siu² joeng⁴

lamp

燈 dang¹

lamp post

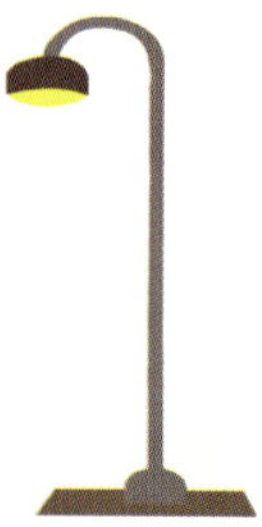

燈柱 dang¹ cyu⁵

land

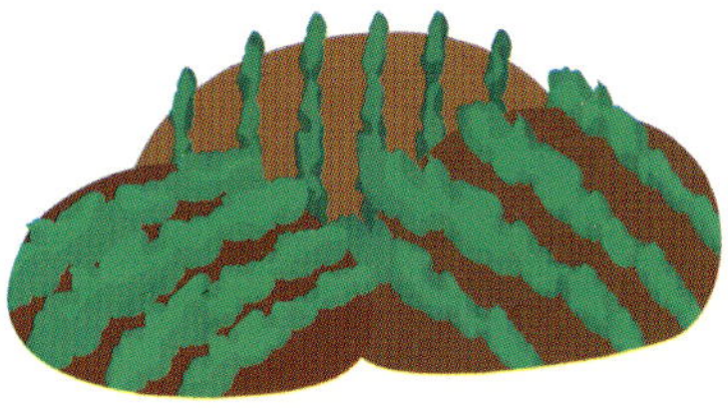

土地 tou² dei⁶

lane

公路 gung¹ lou⁶

lantern

燈籠 dang¹ lung⁴

laser

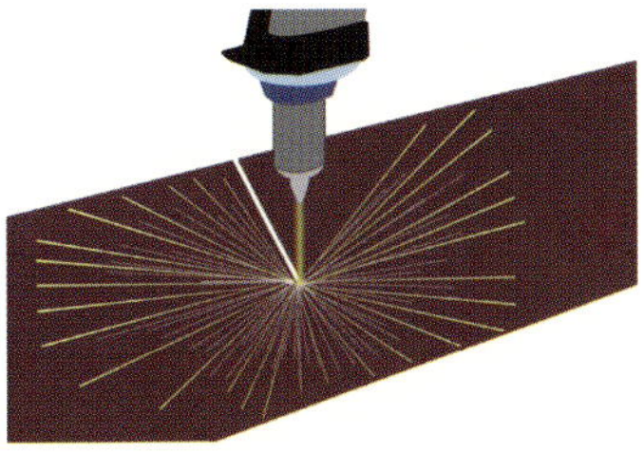

鐳射 leoi⁴ se⁶

lasso

套索 tou³ sok³

latch

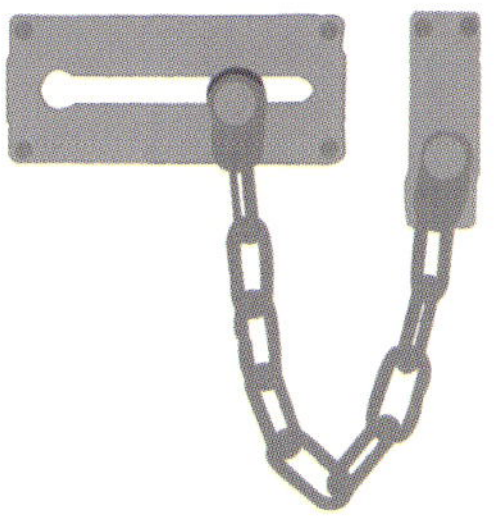

門閂 mun⁴ saan¹

laundry

洗衣物 sai² ji¹ mat⁶

lawn

草地 cou² dei⁶

lawyer

律師 leot⁶ si¹

layer

層 cang⁴

leaf

葉 jip⁶

leather

皮革 pei⁴ gaak³

a b c d e f g h i j k l m n o p q r s t u v w x y z

leg

腿 teoi2

lemon

檸檬 ling4 mung1

lemonade

檸檬汁
ling4 mung1 zap1

lens

鏡片 geng3 pin2

leopard

豹 paau3

letter

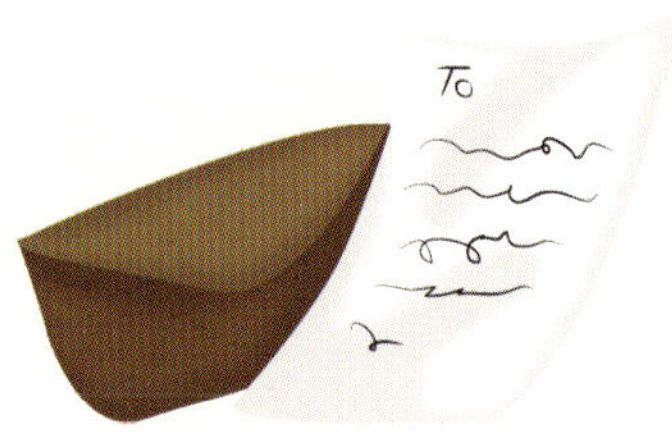

信 seon3

letterbox
US English **mailbox**

信箱 seon3 soeng1

lettuce

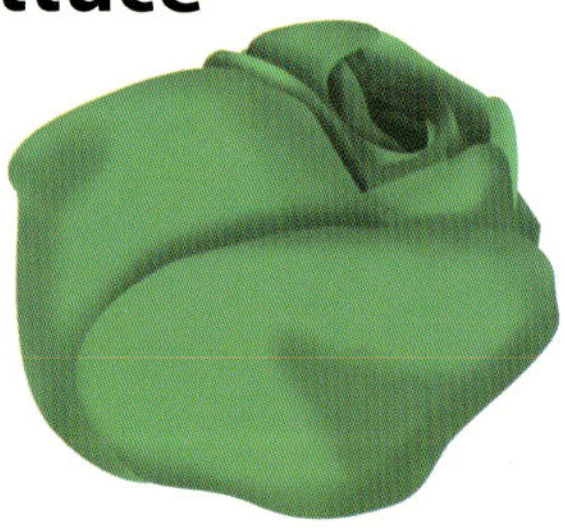

生菜 saang1 coi3

library

圖書館 tou4 syu1 gun2

licence

牌照 paai4 ziu3

lid

蓋 goi3

light

光 gwong1

lighthouse

燈塔 dang^1 taap^3

limb

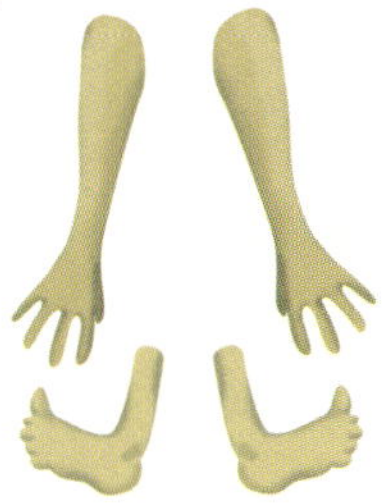

肢體 zi^1 tai^2

line

線 sin^3

lion

獅子 si^1 zi^2

lip

唇 seon^4

lipstick

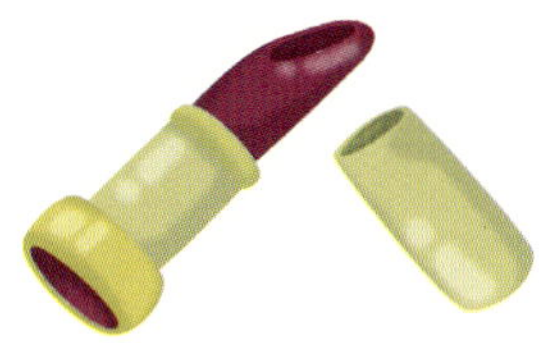

唇膏 seon^4 gou^1

liquid

液體 jik^6 tai^2

list

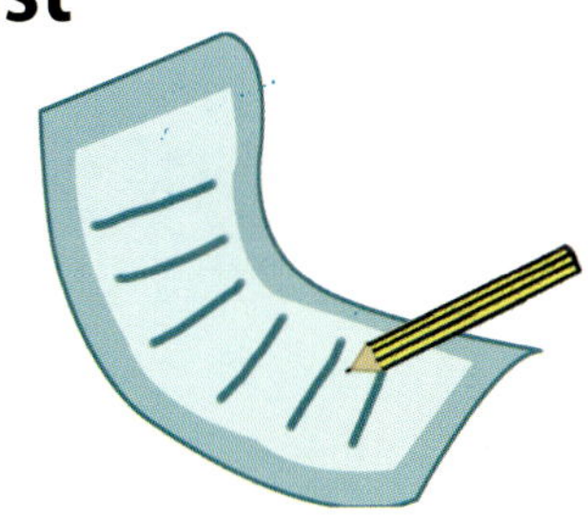

列表 lit^6 biu^2

litre

US English **liter**

公升 gung^1 sing^1

living room

客廳 haak^3 teng^1

lizard

蜥蜴 sik^1 jik^6

load

負荷 fu^6 ho^6

a b c d e f g h i j k l m n o p q r s t u v w x y z

loaf

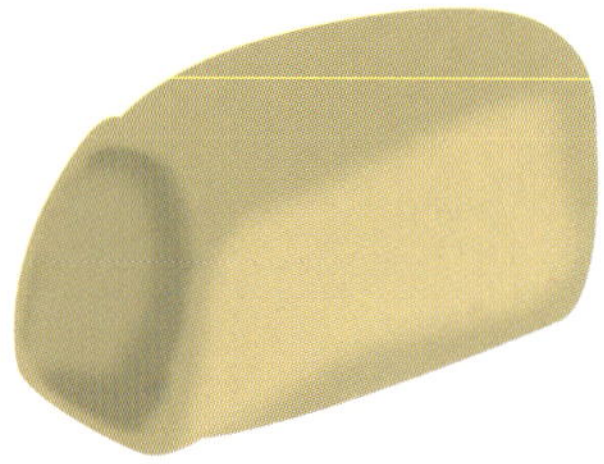

麪包 min6 baau1

lobster

龍蝦 lung4 haa1

lock

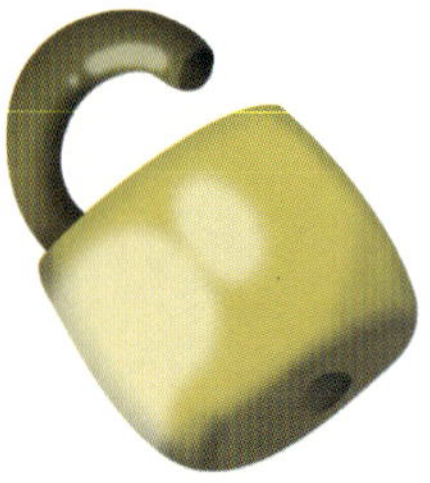

鎖 so2

loft

閣樓 gok3 lau2

log

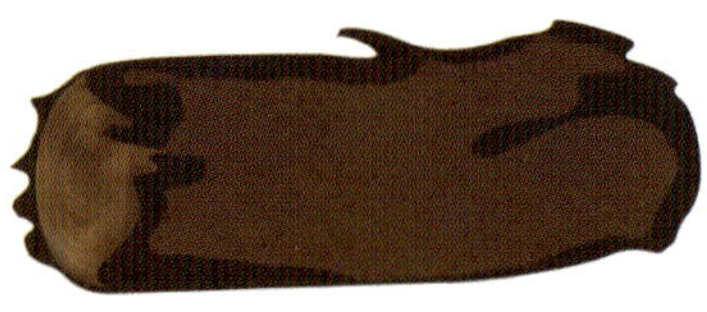

木頭 muk6 tau4

loop

圈 hyun1

lorry
US English **truck**

貨車 fo3 ce1

lotus

蓮花 lin4 faa1

louse

虱 sat1

luggage

行李 hang4 lei5

lunch

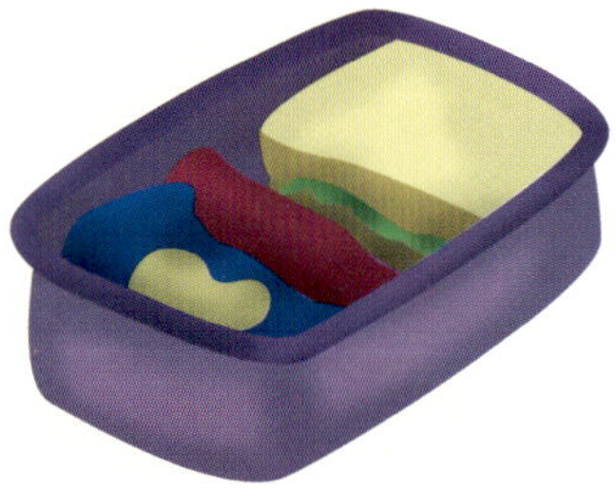

午餐 ng5 caan1

lung

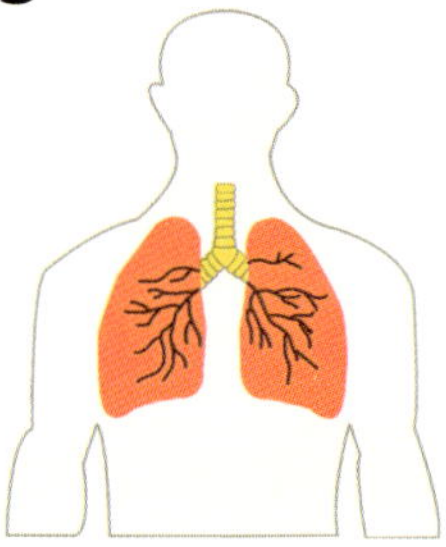

肺 fai3

Mm

machine

機器 gei¹ hei³

magazine

雜誌 zaap⁶ zi³

magician

魔術師 mo¹ seot⁶ si¹

magnet

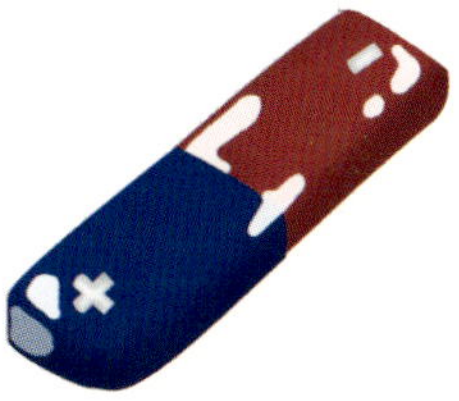

磁石 ci⁴ sek⁶

magpie

喜鵲 hei² coek³

mail

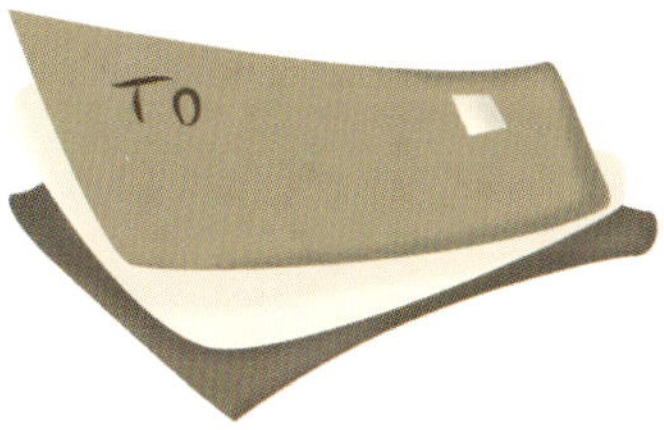

信件 seon³ gin⁶

mammal

哺乳類
bou⁶ jyu⁵ leoi⁶

man

男人 naam⁴ jan²

mandolin

曼陀鈴
maan⁶ to⁴ ling⁴

mango

芒果 mong¹ gwo²

map

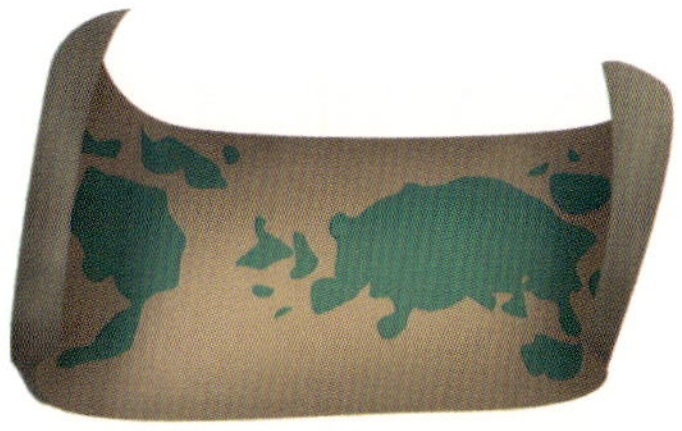

地圖 dei⁶ tou⁴

a b c d e f g h i j k l m n o p q r s t u v w x y z

maple

楓 fung¹

marble

波子 bo¹ zi²

market

市場 si⁵ coeng⁴

mask

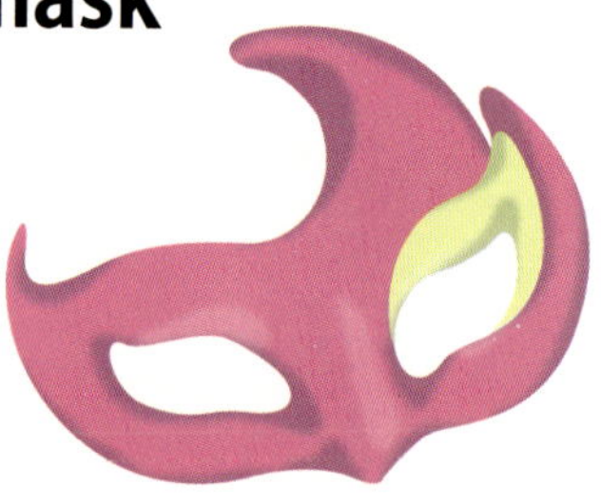

面具 min⁶ geoi⁶

mast

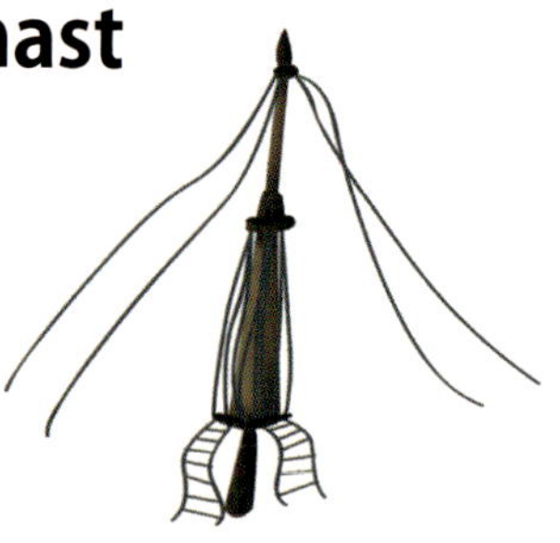

桅杆 wai⁴ gon¹

mat

地墊 dei⁶ zin³

matchbox

火柴盒
fo² caai⁴ hap²

mattress

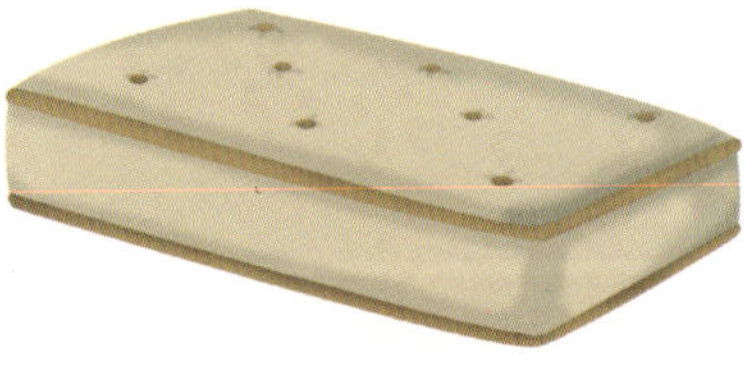

床褥 cong⁴ juk⁶

meal

餐 caan¹

meat

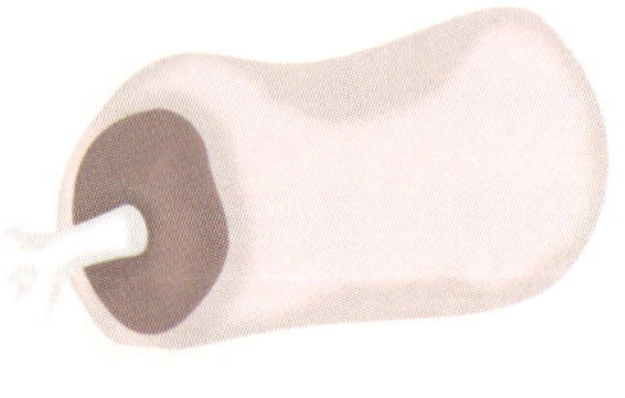

肉 juk⁶

mechanic

機械師 gei¹ haai⁶ si¹

medicine

藥 joek⁶

melon

蜜瓜 mat^{6} gwaa^{1}

merchant

商人 soeng^{1} jan^{4}

mermaid

人魚 jan^{4} jyu^{4}

metal

金屬 gam^{1} suk^{6}

metre

US English **meter**

米 mai^{5}

microphone

咪高峰
mei^{1} gou^{1} fung^{1}

microwave

微波爐
mei^{4} bo^{1} lou^{4}

mile

里 lei^{5}

milk

牛奶 ngau^{4} naai^{5}

miner

礦工 kwong^{3} gung^{1}

mineral

礦物 kwong^{3} mat^{6}

mint

薄荷 bok^{6} ho^{4}

a b c d e f g h i j k l m n o p q r s t u v w x y z

minute

分鐘 fan1 zung1

mirror

鏡 geng3

mobile phone

手提電話 sau2 tai4 din6 waa2

model

模特兒 mou4 dak6 ji4

mole

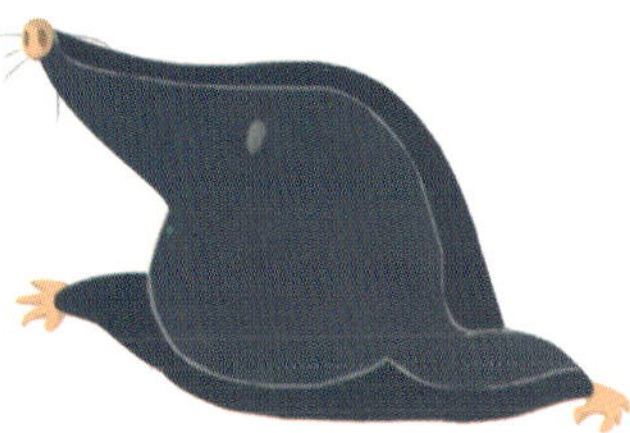

鼴鼠 jin2 syu2

money

錢 cin2

monk

僧人 zang1 jan4

monkey

猴子 hau4 zi2

monster

怪獸 gwaai3 sau3

month

月份 jyut6 fan6

monument

紀念碑 gei2 nim6 bei1

moon

月亮 jyut6 loeng6

mop

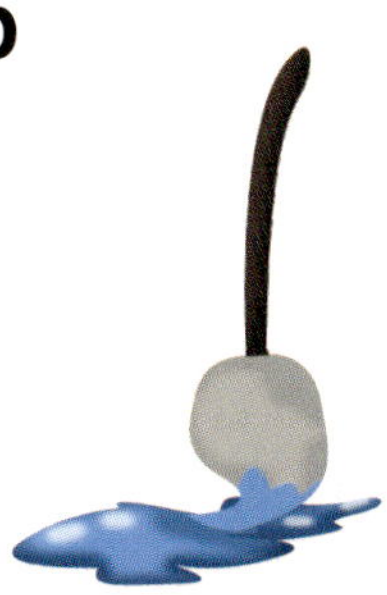

地拖 dei^{6} to^{1}

morning

早上 zou^{2} soeng^{6}

mosquito

蚊子 man^{1} zi^{2}

moth

飛蛾 fei^{1} ngo^{4}

mother

母親 mou^{5} can^{1}

motorcycle

電單車 din^{6} daan^{1} ce^{1}

motorway

高速公路 gou^{1} cuk^{1} gung^{1} lou^{6}

mountain

山 saan^{1}

mouse

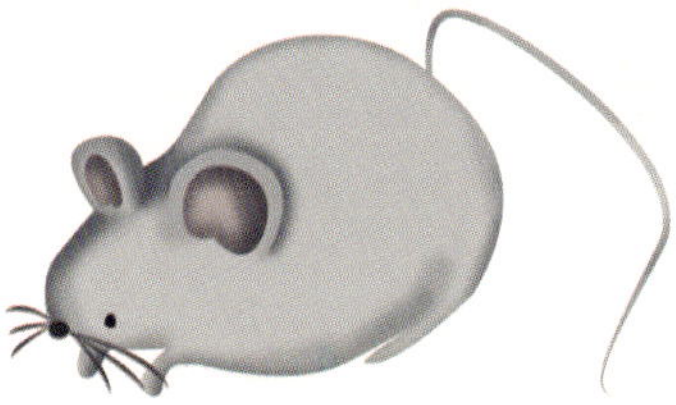

老鼠 lou^{5} syu^{2}

mousetrap

捕鼠器 bou^{6} syu^{2} hei^{3}

moustache

鬍鬚 wu^{4} sou^{1}

mouth

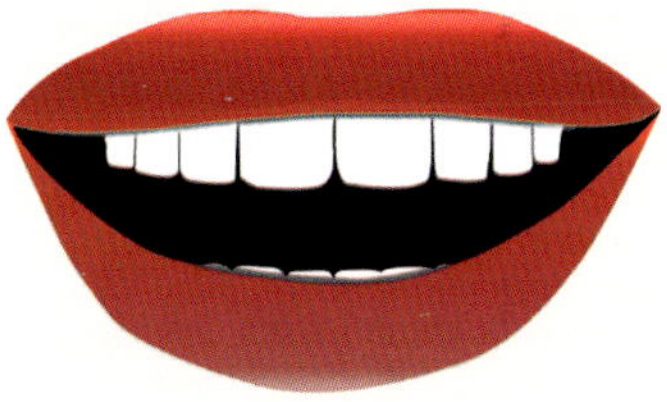

嘴 zeoi^{2}

a b c d e f g h i j k l m n o p q r s t u v w x y z

mud

泥 nai4

muffin

鬆餅 sung1 beng2

mug

杯 bui1

mule

騾 leoi4

muscle

肌肉 gei1 juk6

museum

博物館 bok3 mat6 gun2

mushroom

磨菇 mo4 gu1

music

音樂 jam1 ngok6

musician

音樂家 jam1 ngok6 gaa1

Nn

nail

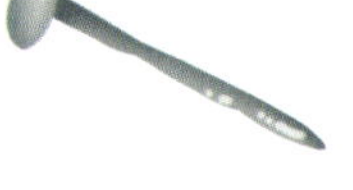

釘 deng1

napkin

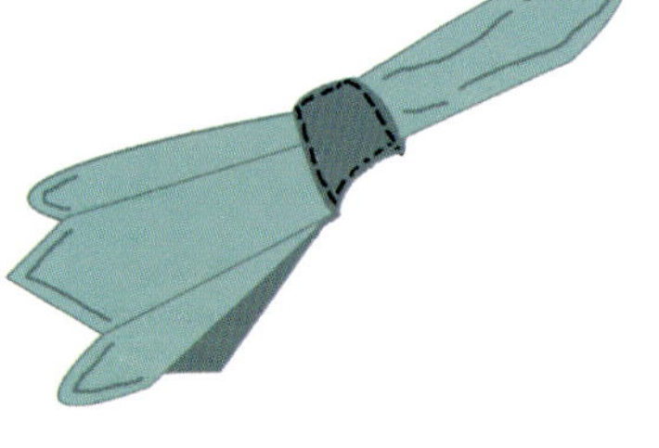

餐巾 caan1 gan1

nappy
US English **diaper**

尿片 niu^6 pin^2

nature

大自然 daai^6 zi^6 jin^4

neck

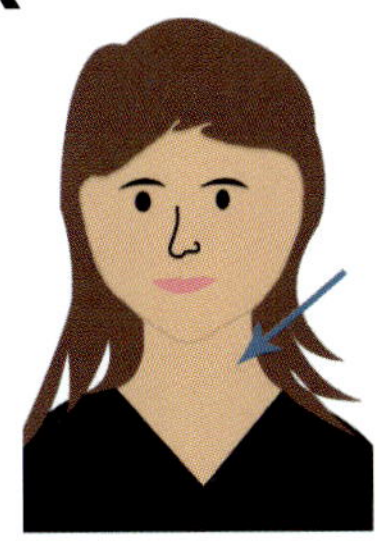

頸 geng^2

necklace

頸鏈 geng^2 lin^2

necktie

領呔 ling^5 taai^1

needle

針 zam^1

neighbour
US English **neighbor**

鄰居 leon^4 geoi^1

nest

雀巢 zoek^3 caau^4

net

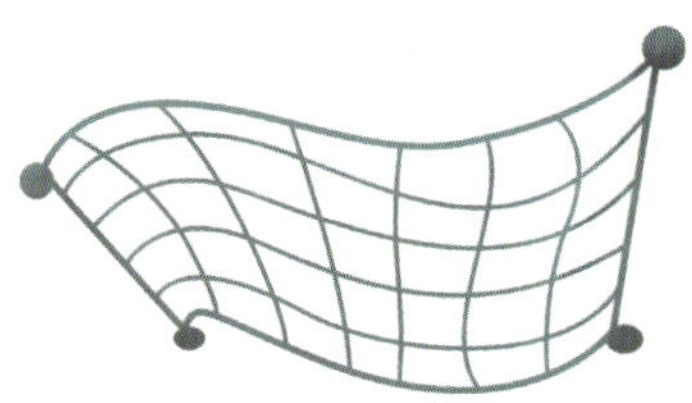

網 mong^5

newspaper

報紙 bou^3 zi^2

night

晚上 maan^5 soeng^6

nine

九 gau^2

noodles

麵 min^{6}

noon

中午 zung^{1} ng^{5}

north

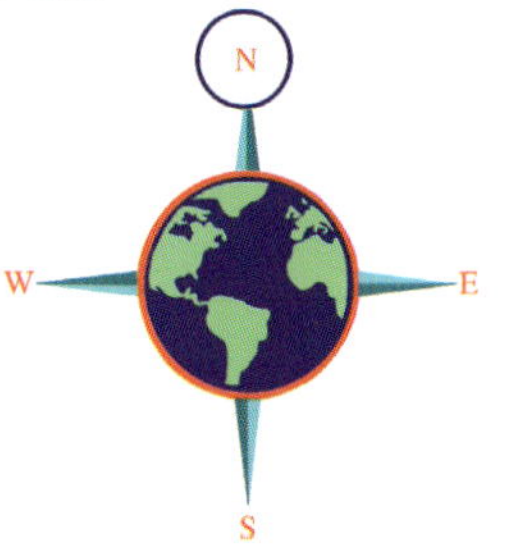

北 bak^{1}

nose

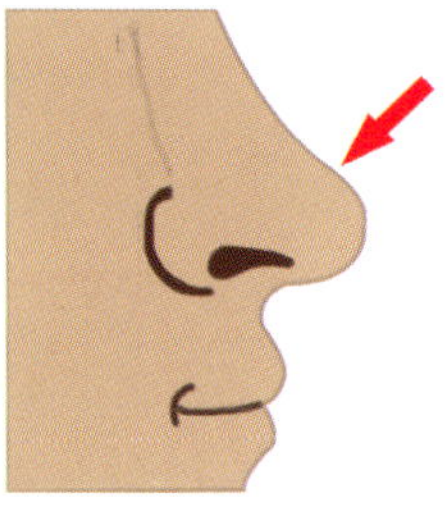

鼻 bei^{6}

note

筆記 bat^{1} gei^{3}

notebook

筆記簿 bat^{1} gei^{3} bou^{2}

notice

告示 gou^{3} si^{6}

number

數字 sou^{3} zi^{6}

nun

修女 sau^{1} neoi^{5}

nurse

護士 wu^{6} si^{6}

nursery

托兒所 tok^{3} ji^{4} so^{2}

nut

堅果 gin^{1} gwo^{2}

Oo

oar

船槳 syun4 zoeng2

observatory

天文台 tin1 man4 toi4

ocean

海洋 hoi2 joeng4

octopus

八爪魚 baat3 zaau2 jyu4

office

辦公室 baan6 gung1 sat1

oil

石油 sek6 jau4

olive

橄欖 gam3 laam5

omelette

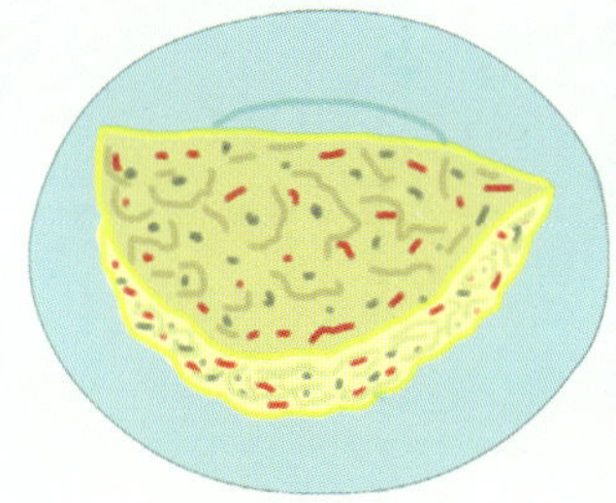

奄列 am1 lit6

one

一 jat1

onion

洋蔥 joeng4 cung1

orange

橙 caang2

orbit

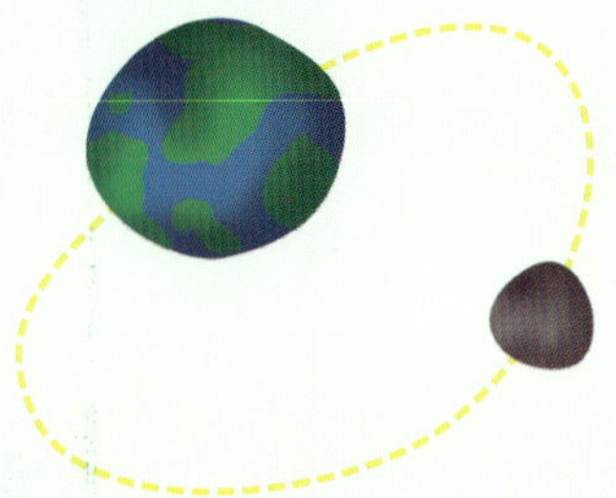

軌道 gwai^{2} dou^{6}

orchard

果園 gwo^{2} jyun^{4}

orchestra

管弦樂團 gun^{2} jin^{4} ngok^{6} tyun^{4}

ostrich

鴕鳥 to^{4} niu^{5}

otter

水獺 seoi^{2} caat^{3}

oval

橢圓 to^{5} jyun^{4}

oven

焗爐 guk^{6} lou^{4}

owl

貓頭鷹 maau^{1} tau^{4} jing^{1}

ox

公牛 gung^{1} ngau^{4}

Pp

packet

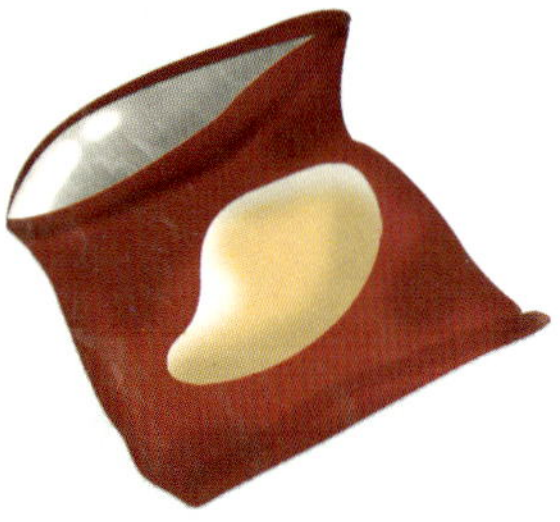

袋裝 doi^{6} zong^{1}

page

書頁 syu^{1} jip^{6}

pain

痛 tung^{3}

paint

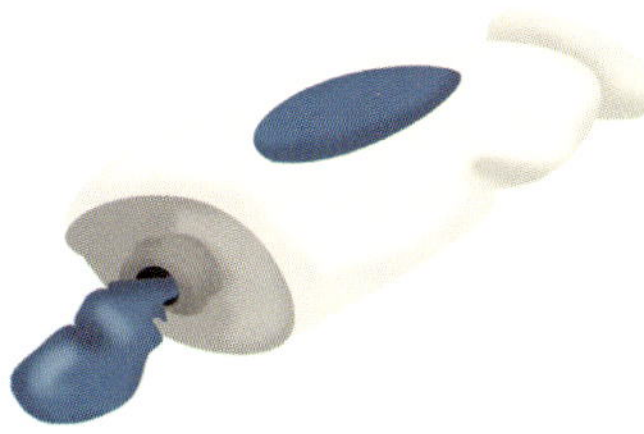

顏料 ngaan^{4} liu^{2}

painting

畫 waa^{2}

pair

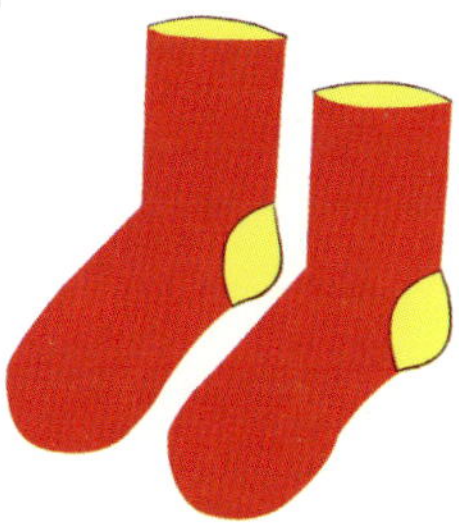

一對 jat^{1} deoi^{3}

palace

皇宮 wong^{4} gung^{1}

palm

手掌 sau^{2} zoeng^{2}

pan

平底鑊
ping^{4} dai^{2} wok^{6}

pancake

班戟 baan^{1} kik^{1}

panda

熊貓 hung^{4} maau^{1}

papaya

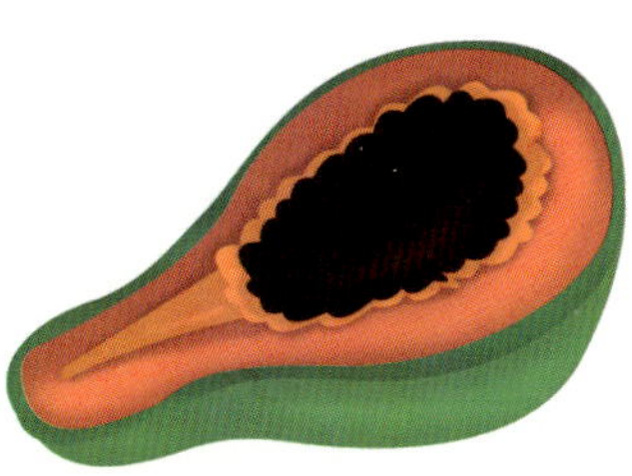

木瓜 muk^{6} gwaa^{1}

paper

紙 zi^{2}

parachute

降落傘
gong^{3} lok^{6} saan^{3}

a b c d e f g h i j k l m n o p q r s t u v w x y z

parcel

包裹 baau^{1} gwo^{2}

park

公園 gung^{1} jyun^{2}

parrot

鸚鵡 jing^{1} mou^{5}

passenger

乘客 sing^{4} haak^{3}

pasta

意粉 ji^{3} fan^{2}

pastry

糕點 gou^{1} dim^{2}

pavement

行人路 hang^{4} jan^{4} lou^{6}

paw

爪 zaau^{2}

pea

青豆 cing^{1} dau^{6}

peach

桃 tou^{4}

peacock

孔雀 hung^{2} zoek^{3}

peak

山頂 saan^{1} deng^{2}

peanut

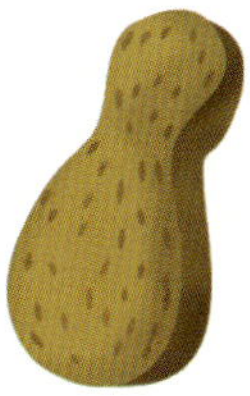

花生 faa1 saang1

pear

梨 lei4

pearl

珍珠 zan1 zyu1

pedal

腳踏 goek3 daap6

pelican

塘鵝 tong4 ngo2

pen

筆 bat1

pencil

鉛筆 jyun4 bat1

penguin

企鵝 kei5 ngo2

pepper

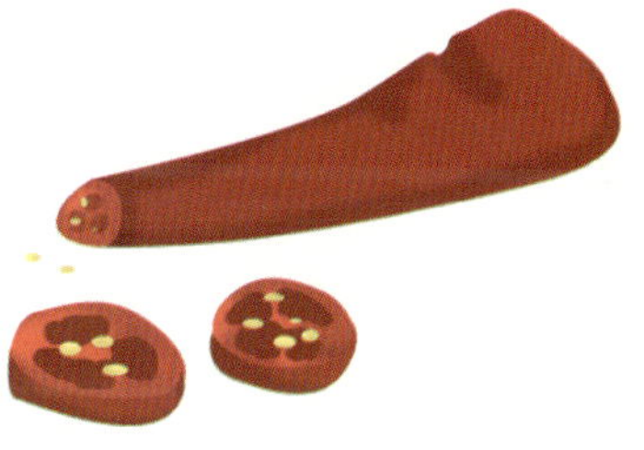

椒 ziu1

perfume

香水 hoeng1 seoi2

pet

寵物 cung2 mat6

pharmacy

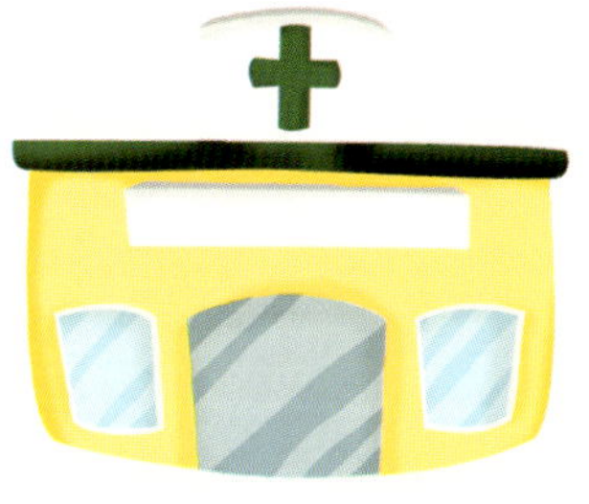

藥房 joek6 fong4

photograph

相片 soeng^{1} pin^{2}

piano

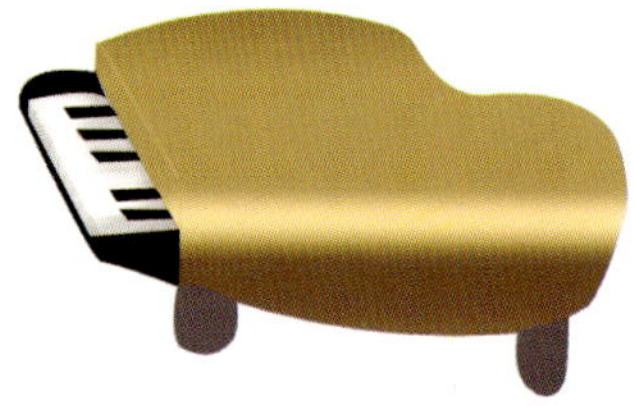

鋼琴 gong^{3} kam^{4}

picture

照片 ziu^{3} pin^{2}

pie

批 pai^{1}

pig

豬 zyu^{1}

pigeon

鴿 gap^{3}

pillar

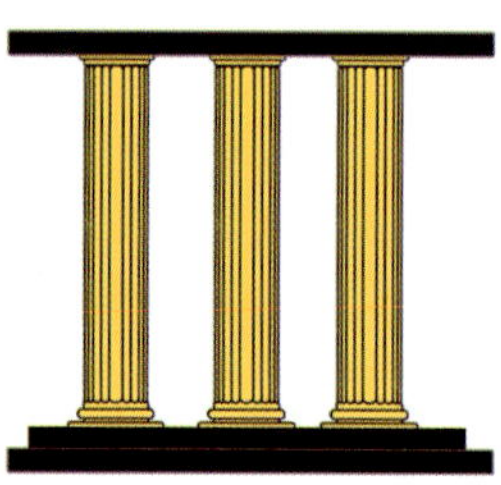

柱 cyu^{5}

pillow

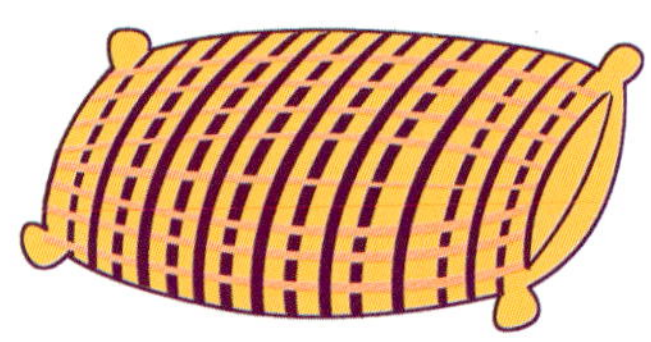

枕頭 zam^{2} tau^{4}

pilot

機師 gei^{1} si^{1}

pineapple

菠蘿 bo^{1} lo^{4}

pink

粉紅色 fan^{2} hung^{4} sik^{1}

pipe

水管 seoi^{2} gun^{2}

pizza  薄餅 bok6 beng2	**planet**  行星 haang4 sing1	**plant**  植物 zik6 mat6
plate  碟 dip6	**platform**  平台 ping4 toi4	**platypus**  鴨嘴獸 ngaap3 zeoi2 sau3
player  玩家 waan6 gaa1	**plum**  布冧 bou3 lam1	**plumber**  水管工 seoi2 gun2 gung1
plywood  夾板 gaap3 baan2	**pocket**  衫袋 saam1 doi2	**poet**  詩人 si1 jan4

a b c d e f g h i j k l m n o p q r s t u v w x y z

polar bear

北極熊
bak1 gik6 hung4

police

警察 ging2 caat3

pollution

污染 wu1 jim5

pomegranate

石榴 sek6 lau4

pond

池塘 ci4 tong4

porcupine

箭豬 zin3 zyu1

port

碼頭 maa5 tau4

porter

行李員
hang4 lei5 jyun4

postcard

明信片
ming4 seon3 pin2

postman

郵差 jau4 caai1

post office

郵局 jau4 guk2

pot

花盆 faa1 pun4

potato

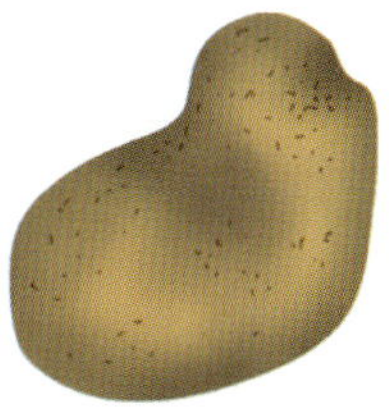

薯仔 syu^4 zai^2

powder

粉末 fan^2 mut^6

prawn

US English **shrimp**

蝦 haa^1

priest

神父 san^4 fu^6

prince

王子 wong^4 zi^2

prison

監獄 gaam^1 juk^6

pudding

布甸 bou^3 din^1

pump

泵 bam^1

pumpkin

南瓜 naam^4 gwaa^1

puppet

木偶 muk^6 ngau^5

puppy

小狗 siu^2 gau^2

purse

銀包 ngan^4 baau^1

Qq

quail

鵪鶉 am¹ seon⁴

quarry

採石場 coi² sek⁶ coeng⁴

queen

王后 wong⁴ hau⁶

queue

排隊 paai⁴ deoi²

quiver

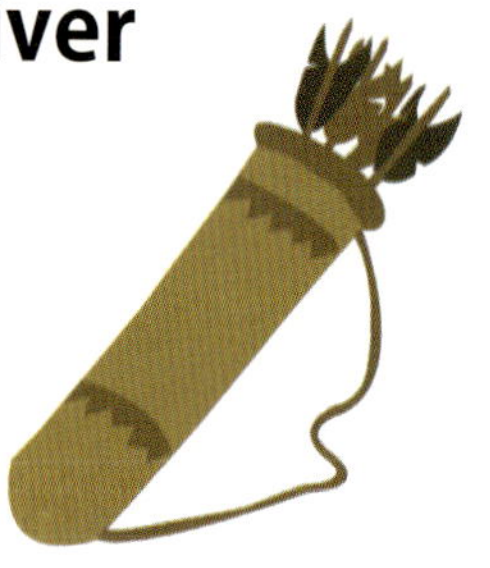

箭筒 zin³ tung²

Rr

rabbit

兔 tou³

rack

架 gaa³

racket

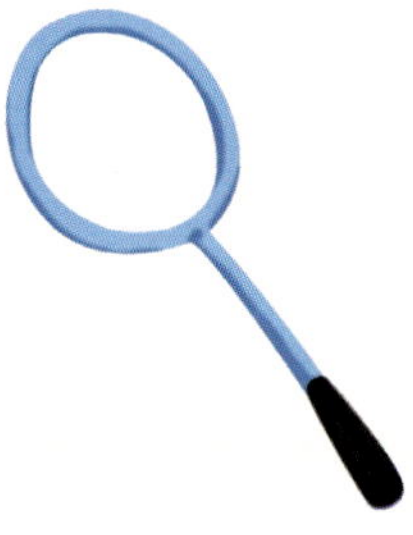

球拍 kau⁴ paak³

radio

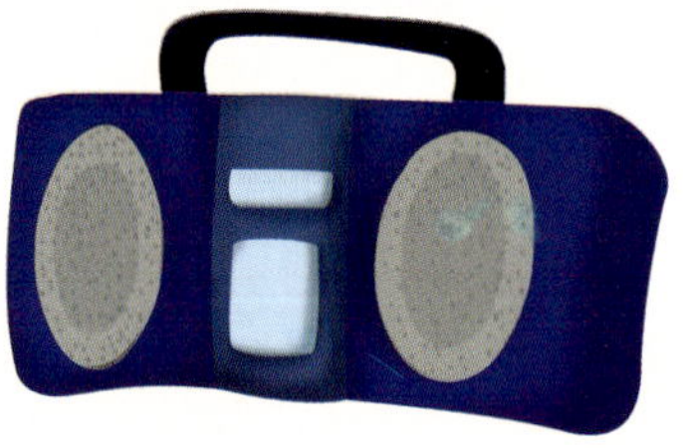

收音機 sau¹ jam¹ gei¹

radish

蘿蔔 lo⁴ baak⁶

raft

木筏 muk^{6} fat^{6}

rain

雨 jyu^{5}

rainbow

彩虹 coi^{2} hung^{4}

raisin

提子乾 tai^{4} zi^{2} gon^{1}

ramp

斜坡 ce^{4} bo^{1}

raspberry

勒士啤梨
lak^{6} si^{6} be^{1} lei^{2}

rat

老鼠 lou^{5} syu^{2}

razor

剃刀 tai^{3} dou^{1}

receipt

收據 sau^{1} geoi^{3}

rectangle

長方形
coeng^{4} fong^{1} jing^{4}

red

紅色 hung^{4} sik^{1}

restaurant

餐廳 caan^{1} teng^{1}

rhinoceros

犀牛 sai^1 ngau^4

rib

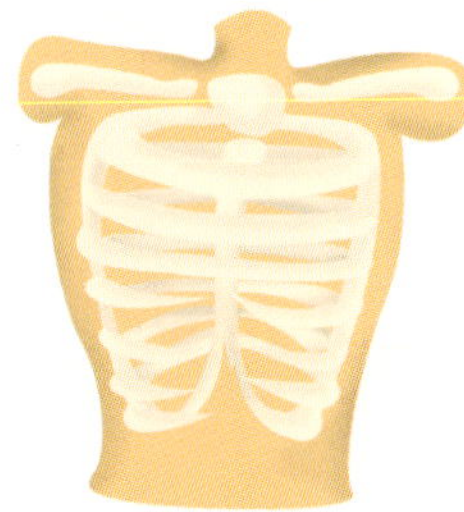

肋骨 laak^6 gwat^1

ribbon

絲帶 si^1 daai^2

rice

米飯 mai^5 faan^6

ring

戒指 gaai^3 zi^2

river

河 ho^4

road

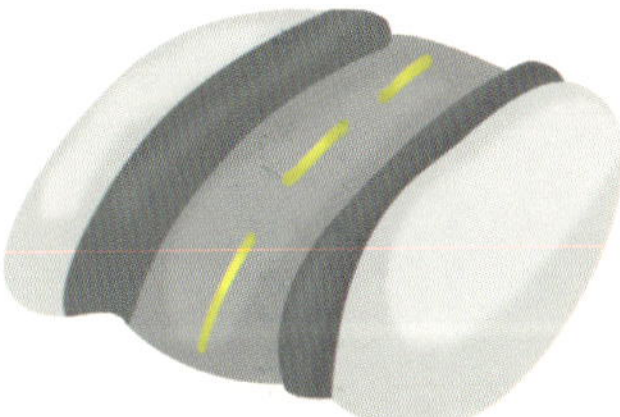

馬路 maa^5 lou^6

robber

盜賊 dou^6 caak^3

robe

袍 pou^4

robot

機械人 gei^1 haai^6 jan^4

rock

石 sek^6

rocket

火箭 fo^2 zin^3

roller coaster

過山車
gwo3 saan1 ce1

room

房間 fong4 gaan1

root

根 gan1

rope

繩 sing4

rose

玫瑰 mui4 gwai3

round

圓 jyun4

rug

地氈 dei6 zin1

rugby

欖球 laam2 kau4

ruler

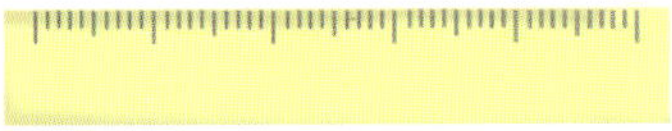

間尺 gaan3 cek2

Ss

sack

布袋 bou3 doi2

sail

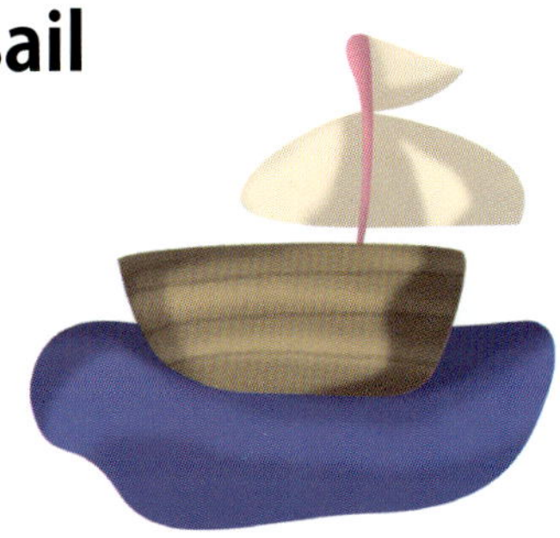

航行 hong4 hang4

sailor

水手 seoi2 sau2

salad

沙律 saa1 leot2

salt

鹽 jim4

sand

沙 saa1

sandwich

三文治
saam1 man4 zi6

satellite

人造衛星
jan4 zou6 wai6 sing1

saucer

茶碟 caa4 dip6

sausage

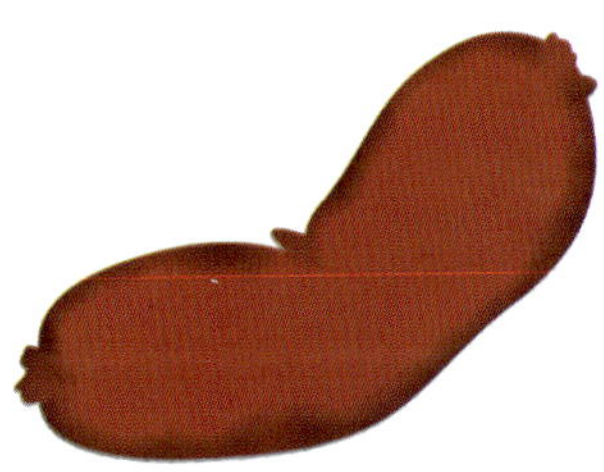

香腸 hoeng1 coeng2

saw

鋸 goe3

scarf

頸巾 geng2 gan1

school

學校 hok6 haau6

scissors

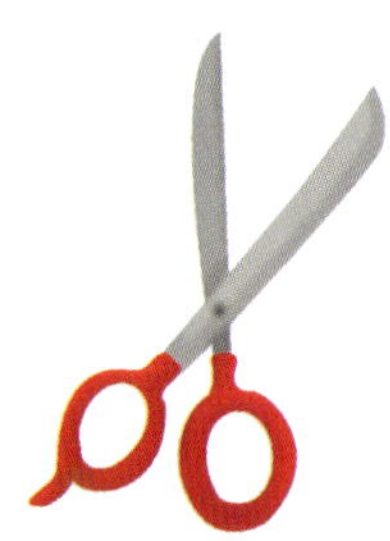

鉸剪 gaau2 zin2

scooter

滑板車
waat6 baan2 ce1

scorpion

蠍子 kit3 zi2

screw

螺絲 lo4 si1

sea

海 hoi2

seal

海豹 hoi2 paau3

seat

座位 zo6 wai2

see-saw

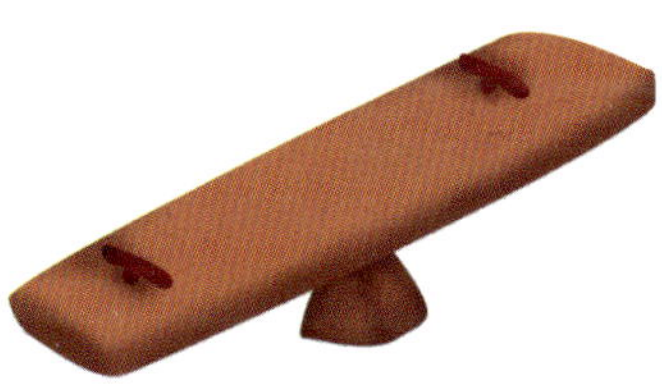

搖搖板
jiu4 jiu4 baan2

seven

七 cat1

shadow

影子 jing2 zi2

shampoo

洗頭水
sai2 tau4 seoi2

shark

鯊魚 saa1 jyu2

sheep

綿羊 min4 joeng2

shelf

書架 syu^1 gaa^2

shell

貝殼 bui^3 hok^3

shelter

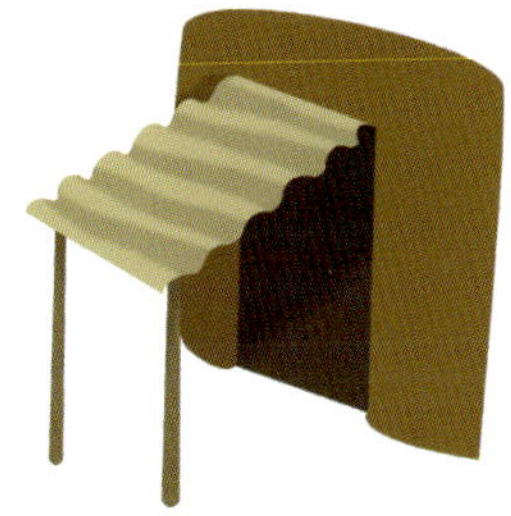

遮蔭處 ze^1 jam^1 cyu^3

ship

船 syun^4

shirt

恤衫 seot^1 saam^1

shoe

鞋 haai^4

shorts

短褲 dyun^2 fu^3

shoulder

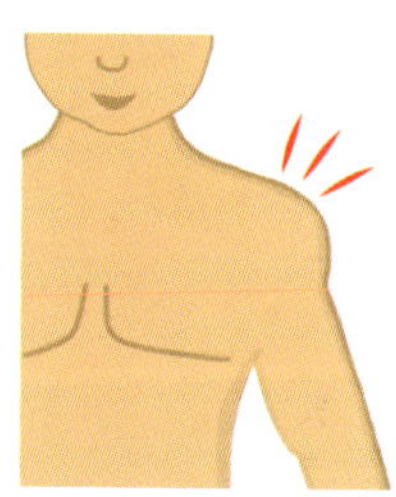

膊 bok^3

shower

淋浴 lam^4 juk^6

shutter

百葉窗 baak^3 jip^6 coeng^1

shuttlecock

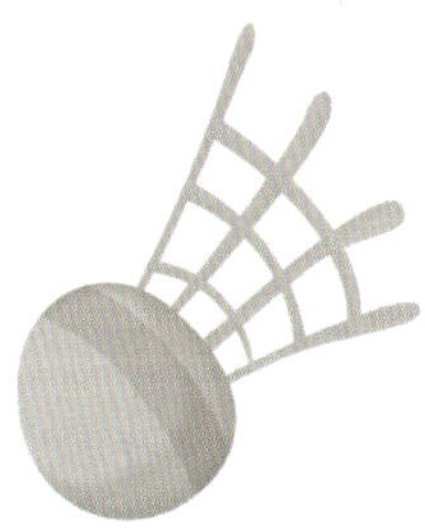

羽毛球 jyu^5 mou^4 kau^4

signal

紅綠燈 hung^4 luk^6 dang^1

silver

銀 ngan^4

sink

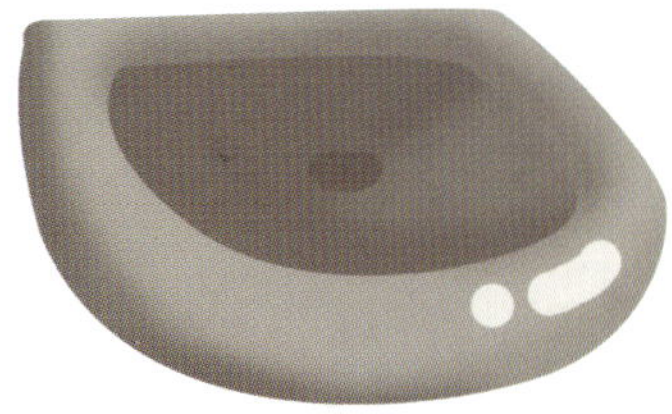

鉼盆 sing^1 pun^2

sister

姊妹 zi^2 mui^6

six

六 luk^6

skate

溜冰 lau^4 bing^1

skeleton

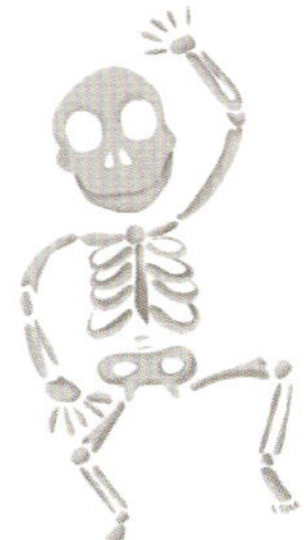

骷髏骨
fu^1 lau^4 gwat^1

ski

滑雪 waat^6 syut^3

skin

皮膚 pei^4 fu^1

skirt

短裙
dyun^2 kwan^4

skull

骷髏頭
fu^1 lou^4 tau^4

sky

天空 tin^1 hung^1

skyscraper

摩天大廈
mo^1 tin^1 daai^6 haa^6

slide

滑梯 waat^{6} tai^{1}

slipper

拖鞋 to^{1} haai^{2}

smoke

煙 jin^{1}

snail

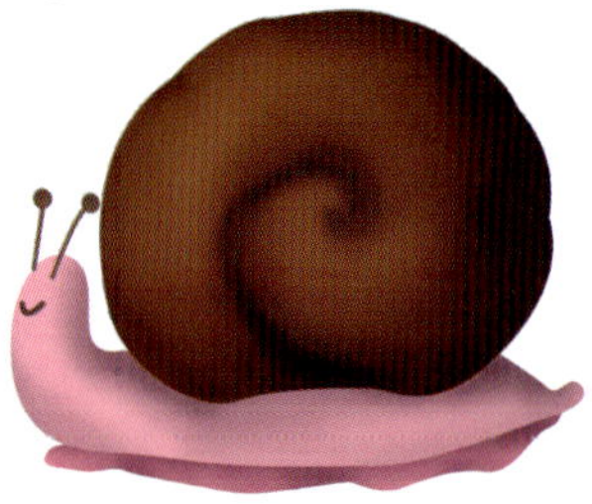

蝸牛 wo^{1} ngau^{4}

snake

蛇 se^{4}

snow

雪 syut^{3}

soap

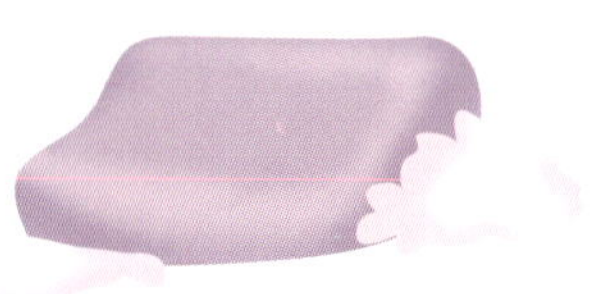

番梘 faan^{1} gaan^{2}

sock

襪 mat^{6}

sofa

梳化 so^{1} faa^{2}

soil

泥土 nai^{4} tou^{2}

soldier

士兵 si^{6} bing^{1}

soup

湯 tong^{1}

space

太空 taai^{3} hung^{1}

spaghetti

意粉 ji^{3} fan^{2}

sphere

球體 kau^{4} tai^{2}

spider

蜘蛛 zi^{1} zyu^{1}

spinach

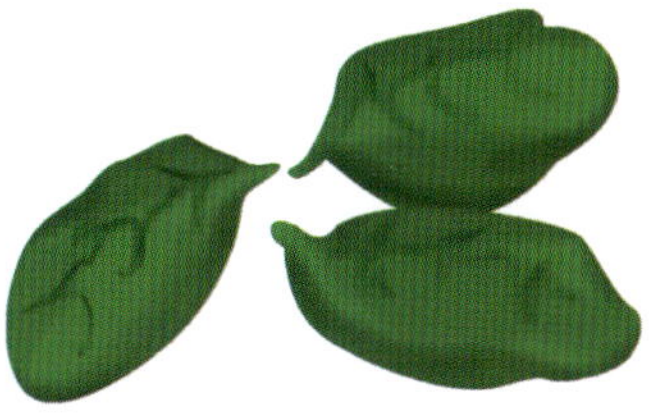

菠菜 bo^{1} coi^{3}

sponge

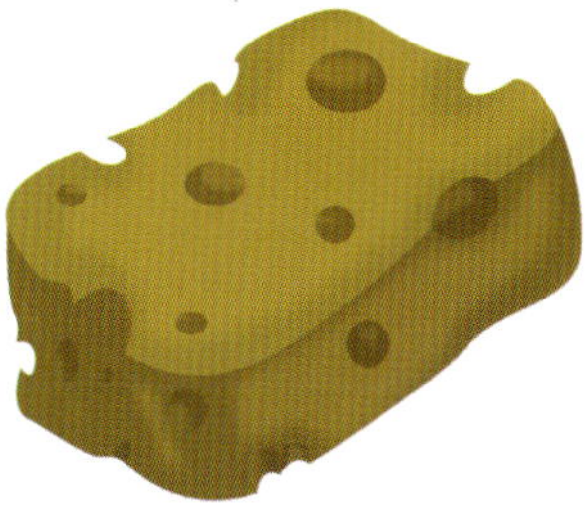

海綿 hoi^{2} min^{4}

spoon

匙羹 ci^{4} gang^{1}

spray

噴霧 pan^{3} mou^{6}

spring

春天 ceon^{1} tin^{1}

square

正方形
zing^{3} fong^{1} jing^{4}

squirrel

松鼠 cung^{4} syu^{2}

stadium

體育館
tai^{2} juk^{6} gun^{2}

stairs

樓梯 lau^{4} tai^{1}

stamp

郵票 jau^{4} piu^{3}

star

星 sing^{1}

station

車站 ce^{1} zaam^{6}

statue

雕像 diu^{1} zoeng^{6}

stethoscope

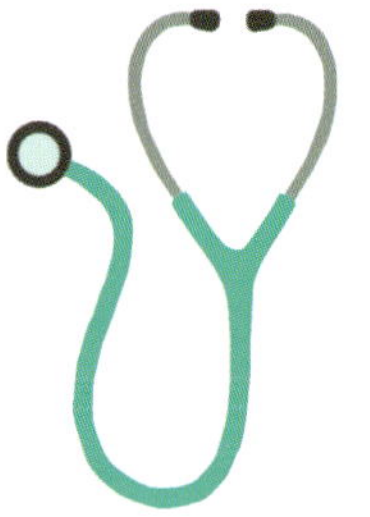

聽筒 teng^{1} tung^{2}

stomach

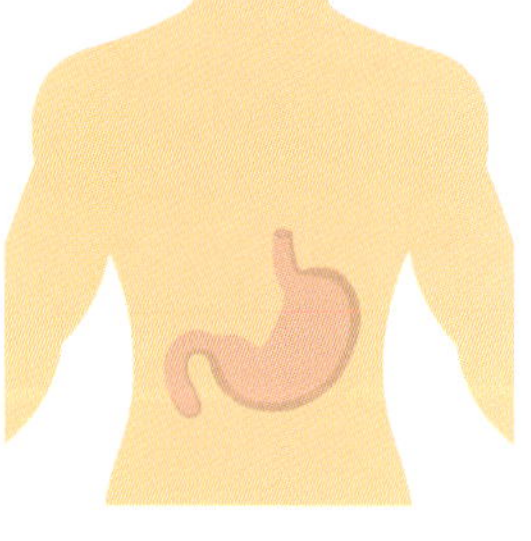

胃 wai^{6}

stone

石頭 sek^{6} tau^{4}

storm

暴風雨 bou^{6} fung^{1} jyu^{5}

straw

飲管 jam^{2} gun^{2}

strawberry

士多啤梨 si^{6} do^{1} be^{1} lei^{2}

street

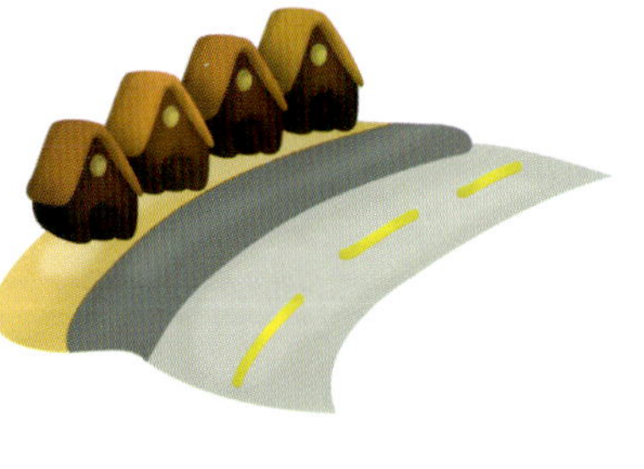

街道 gaai^{1} dou^{6}

student

學生 hok⁶ saang¹

submarine

潛水艇
cim⁴ seoi² teng⁵

subway

地鐵 dei⁶ tit³

sugar

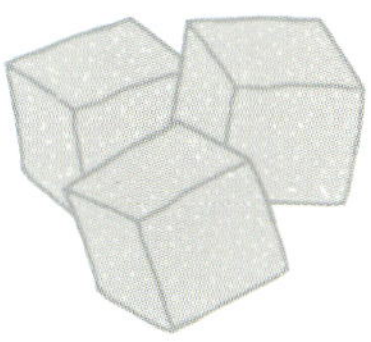

糖 tong⁴

sugarcane

甘蔗 gam¹ ze³

summer

夏天 haa⁶ tin¹

sun

太陽 taai³ joeng⁴

supermarket

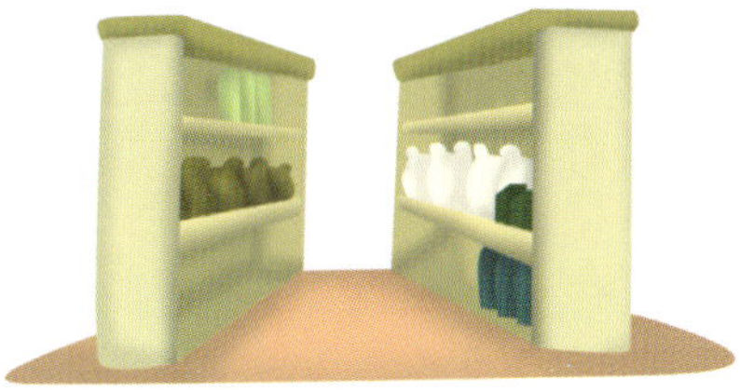

超級市場
ciu¹ kap¹ si⁵ coeng⁴

swan

天鵝 tin¹ ngo⁴

sweet

糖果 tong⁴ gwo²

swimming pool

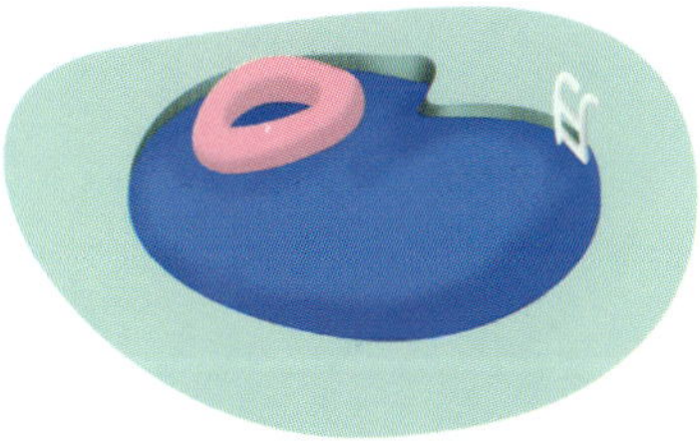

泳池 wing⁶ ci⁴

swimsuit

泳衣 wing⁶ ji¹

a b c d e f g h i j k l m n o p q r s t u v w x y z

swing

韆鞦 cin^1 cau^1

switch

電掣 din^6 zai^3

syrup

糖漿 tong^4 zoeng^1

Tt

table

桌子 coek^3 zi^2

tall

高 gou^1

tank

坦克車 taan^2 hak^1 ce^1

taxi

的士 dik^1 si^2

tea

茶 caa^4

teacher

教師 gaau^3 si^1

teeth

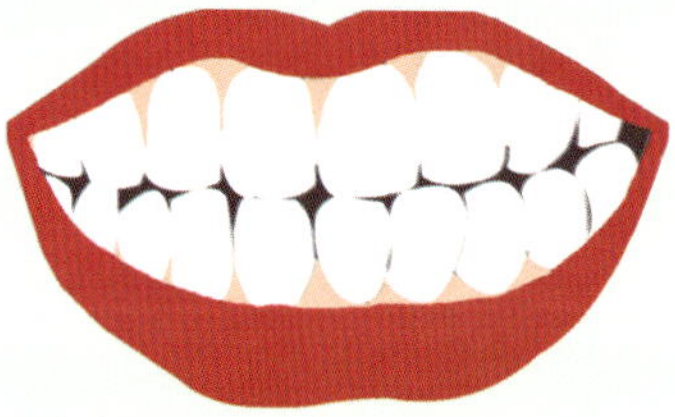

牙齒 ngaa^4 ci^2

telephone

電話 din^6 waa^2

television

電視 din6 si6

ten

十 sap6

tennis

網球 mong5 kau4

tent

帳篷 zoeng3 pung4

thief

小偷 siu2 tau1

thread

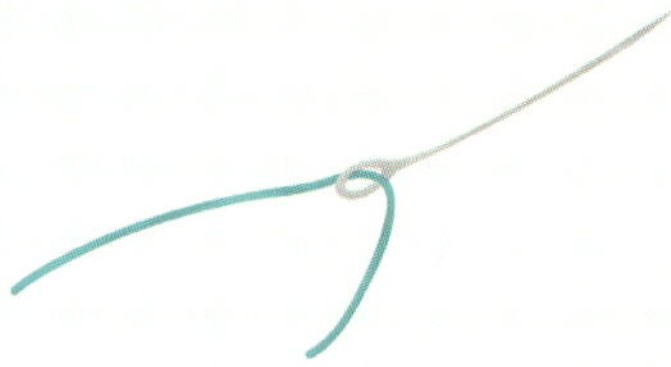

線 sin3

three

三 saam1

throat

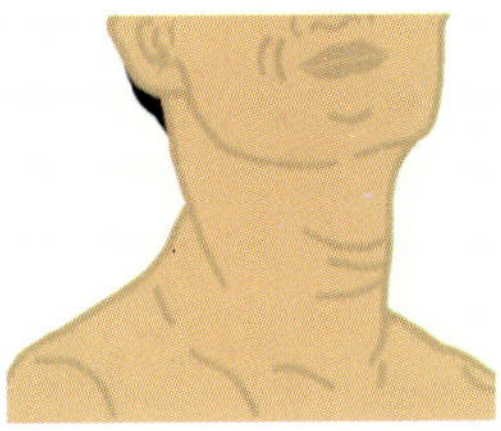

喉嚨 hau4 lung4

thumb

拇指 mou5 zi2

ticket

票 piu3

tiger

老虎 lou5 fu2

toe

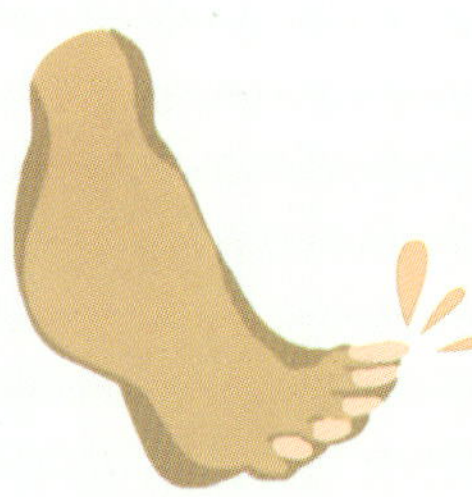

腳趾 goek3 zi2

tofu

豆腐 dau6 fu6

tomato

番茄 faan4 ke2

tongue

舌頭 sit3 tau4

tool

工具 gung1 geoi6

toothbrush

牙刷 ngaa4 caat2

toothpaste

牙膏 ngaa4 gou1

tortoise

烏龜 wu1 gwai1

towel

毛巾 mou4 gan1

tower

塔 taap3

toy

玩具 wun6 geoi6

tractor

拖拉機 to1 laai1 gei1

train

火車 fo2 ce1

tree

樹 syu^{6}

triangle

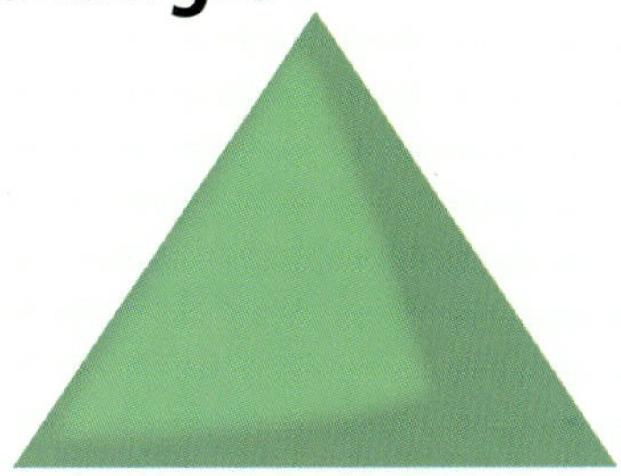

三角形
saam^{1} gok^{3} jing^{4}

tub

浴缸 juk^{6} gong^{1}

tunnel

隧道 seoi^{6} dou^{6}

turnip

大頭菜
daai^{6} tau^{4} coi^{3}

tyre
US English **tire**

車呔 ce^{1} taai^{1}

Uu

umbrella

雨傘 jyu^{5} saan^{3}

uncle

叔叔 suk^{1} suk^{1}

uniform

制服 zai^{3} fuk^{6}

university

大學 daai^{6} hok^{6}

utensil

餐具 caan^{1} geoi^{6}

a b c d e f g h i j k l m n o p q r s t u v w x y z

Vv

vacuum cleaner

吸塵機 kap^{1} can^{4} gei^{1}

valley

山谷 saan^{1} guk^{1}

van

小巴 siu^{2} baa^{1}

vase

花樽 faa^{1} zeon^{1}

vault

保險庫 bou^{2} him^{2} fu^{3}

vegetable

蔬菜 so^{1} coi^{3}

veil

面紗 min^{6} saa^{1}

vet

獸醫 sau^{3} ji^{1}

village

村莊 cyun^{1} zong^{1}

violet

紫色 zi^{2} sik^{1}

violin

小提琴 siu^{2} tai^{4} kam^{4}

volcano

火山 fo² saan¹

volleyball

排球 paai⁴ kau⁴

vulture

禿鷲 tuk¹ zau⁶

Ww

waist

腰 jiu¹

waitress

女侍應 neoi⁵ si⁶ jing³

wall

牆壁 coeng⁴ bik¹

wallet

銀包 ngan⁴ baau¹

walnut

合桃 hap⁶ tou⁴

wand

魔杖 mo¹ zoeng⁶

wardrobe

衣櫃 ji¹ gwai⁶

warehouse
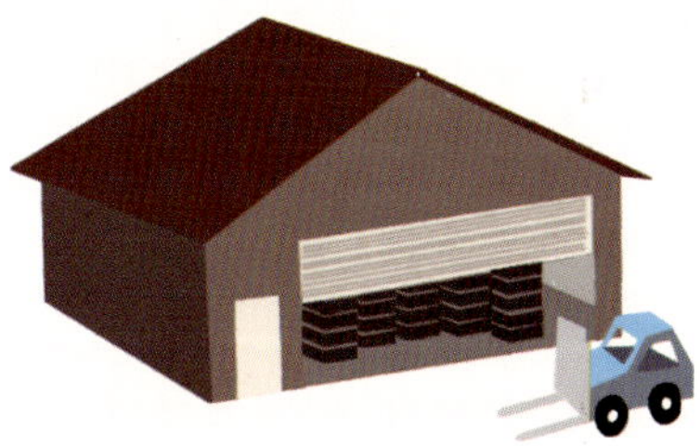

倉庫 cong¹ fu³

wasp

黃蜂 wong^{4} fung^{1}

watch

手錶 sau^{2} biu^{1}

water

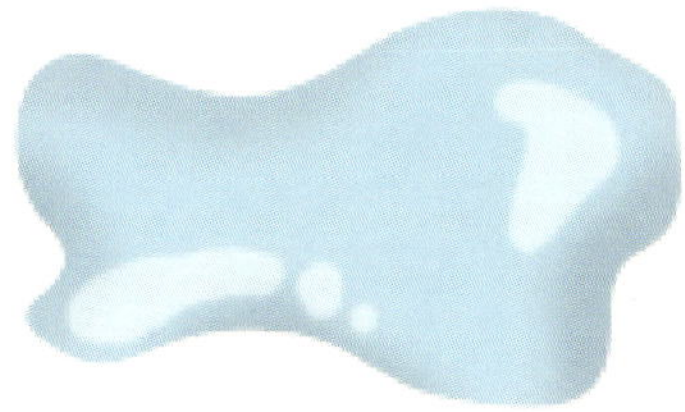

水 seoi^{2}

watermelon

西瓜 sai^{1} gwaa^{1}

web

蜘蛛網 zi^{1} zyu^{1} mong^{5}

whale

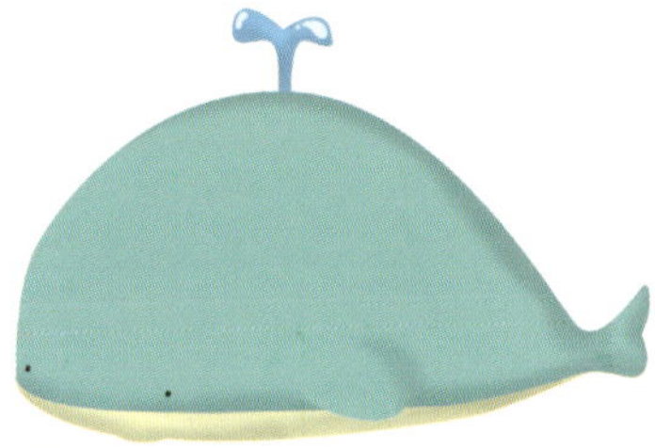

鯨魚 king^{4} jyu^{4}

wheat

小麥 siu^{2} mak^{6}

wheel

車輪 ce^{1} leon^{4}

whistle

哨子 saau^{3} zi^{2}

white

白色 baak^{6} sik^{1}

wife

妻子 cai^{1} zi^{2}

window

窗 coeng^{1}

wing

翼 jik^{6}

winter

冬天 dung^{1} tin^{1}

wizard

巫師 mou^{4} si^{1}

wolf

狼 long^{4}

woman

女人 neoi^{5} jan^{4}

woodpecker

啄木鳥 doek^{3} muk^{6} niu^{5}

wool

羊毛 joeng^{4} mou^{4}

workshop

工作坊 gung^{1} zok^{3} fong^{1}

wrist

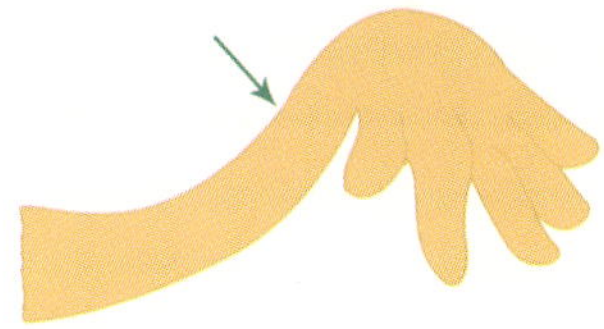

手腕 sau^{2} wun^{2}

Xx

x-ray

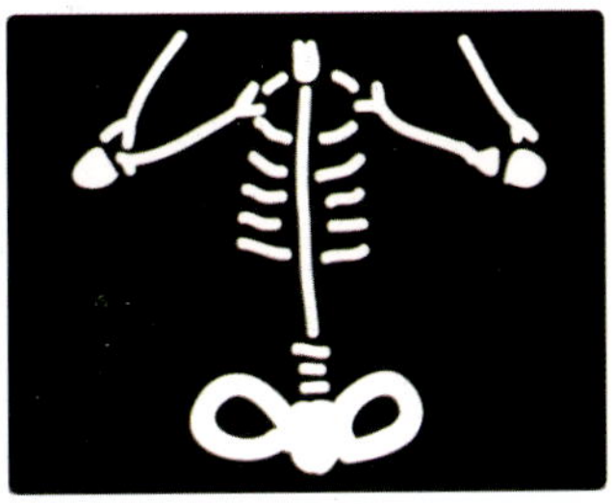

X光 ik^{1} si^{4} gwong^{1}

xylophone

木琴 muk^{6} kam^{4}

Yy

yacht

帆船 faan^{4} syun^{4}

yak

犛牛 lei^{4} ngau^{4}

yard

花園 faa^{1} jyun^{2}

yellow

黃色 wong^{4} sik^{1}

yoghurt

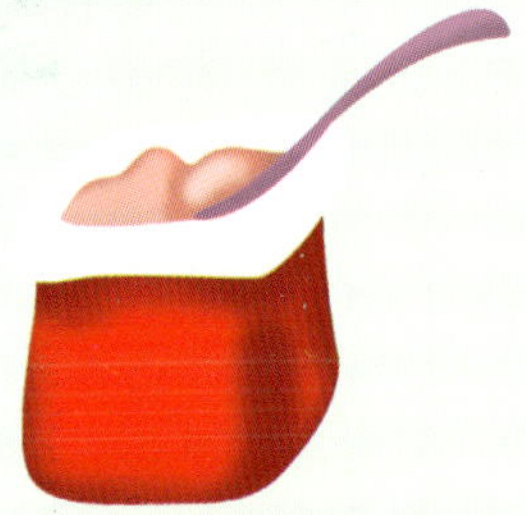

乳酪 jyu^{5} lok^{3}

Zz

zebra

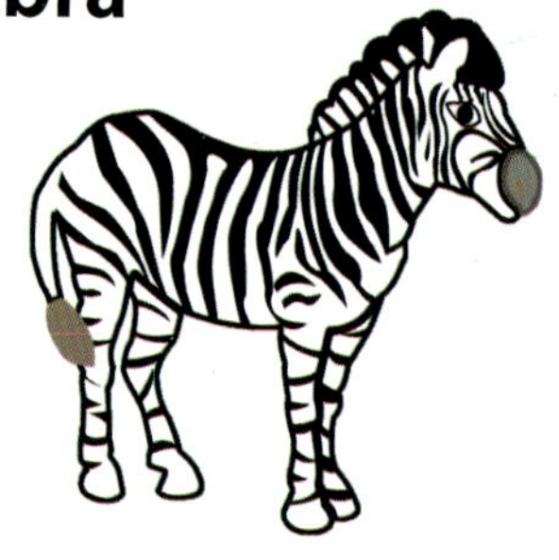

斑馬 baan^{1} maa^{5}

zero

零 ling^{4}

zip

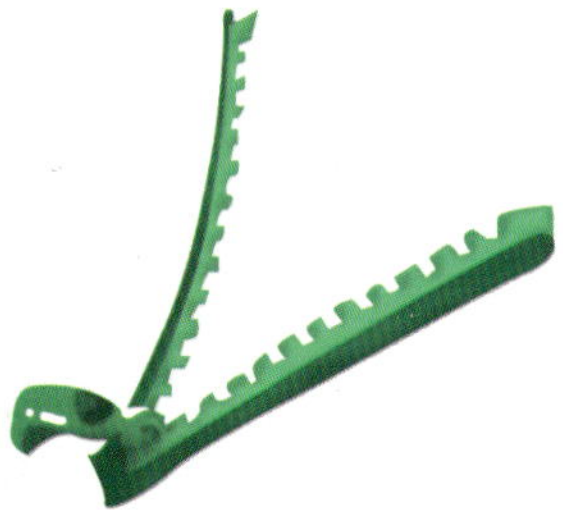

拉鏈 laai^{1} lin^{2}

zodiac

星座 sing^{1} zo^{6}

zoo

動物園
dung^{6} mat^{6} jyun^{4}